FACILITATING FOR GROWTH

A Guide for Scripture Study Groups and Small Christian Communities

Barbara J. Fleischer

A Liturgical Press Book

 THE LITURGICAL PRESS
Collegeville, Minnesota

1   2   3   4   5   6   7   8   9

Library of Congress Cataloging-in-Publication Data

Fleischer, Barbara J.
    Facilitating for growth : a guide for Scripture study groups and
small Christian communities / Barbara J. Fleischer.
        p.   cm.
    ISBN 0-8146-2170-8
    1. Church group work. 2. Group relations training. 3. Social
facilitation. 4. Small groups. 5. Bible—Study and teaching.
6. Christian communities—Catholic Church. I. Title.
BV652.2.F54   1993
253'.7—dc20   93-1341
                                                                CIP

CONTENTS

PART B: WORKSHOP SESSIONS

INTRODUCTION

The verb "facilitate" means "to make easy." In the context of small groups, the facilitator makes easy the work of the group, enabling members to accomplish the task they set before themselves and to enjoy the time they spend together. For groups who gather to study Scripture or other theological texts, the facilitator guides participants in their explorations and reflections, helping members share their thoughts, feelings, actions, and deepening prayer life with one another. Nourishing the group's spirit of joy is also an important part of the facilitator's calling.

The purpose of this book is also to facilitate, to make easy the development of knowledge and skills that can help small group facilitators become more confident and effective in their work with groups. Great facilitators are not born with their abilities; they develop them. Effective facilitators know what to look for in observing group process. They can articulate their ideas clearly and help others name their experiences and insights. They challenge others to think more deeply about perceptions and initial observations. The wonderful news for anyone who would like to be a small-group facilitator is that these skills can be learned and sharpened with practice.

The content and exercises of each chapter in this book present practical information and methods to help facilitators deepen their knowledge of their role and hone their skills in group facilitation. While developed primarily for use with the Little Rock Scripture Study, the skills presented here may be applicable to the development of facilitation skills for a variety of faith-sharing approaches.

The material is in two major sections. Part A offers eight chapters on various aspects of facilitation. Each chapter begins with "Warm-Up Exercises" consisting of questions and assignments designed to help readers draw from their own experience as they dialogue with the written material presented in each chapter.

Part B presents an outline for eight ninety-minute workshop sessions, corresponding to the eight topics introduced in Part A. The eight sessions represent twelve hours of training time that can be structured into various formats: eight ninety-minute sessions, four three-hour sessions, or a two-day workshop. Single sessions may also be used independently as each parish or community identifies its needs. Experiential exercises for developing and practicing skills essential for artful and effective facilitating form the heart of the facilitator training program presented in Part B.

HOW TO USE THIS BOOK

This book is primarily intended for those who will participate in a series of workshops aimed at helping participants gain greater ease and skill in facilitating Scripture study groups. Generally, each workshop session should have a minimum of six participants and at least one "workshop coordinator" for every twelve participants. The workshop coordinator's role is to facilitate the group in moving through the session learning designs presented in Part B.

In order to take part fully in the workshop sessions, participants should complete all assignments and readings presented in the appropriate chapter(s) in Part A before coming to the session. Thus, if the parish or sponsoring group is combining Session 1 and 2 into one evening, participants should complete all assignments in Chapters 1 and 2 before coming to the workshop.

Part B provides the session design and additional materials that will be used during the workshop session itself. Workshop coordinators should review the session design well in advance of the workshop date to gather all materials needed.

ACKNOWLEDGEMENTS

I want to express my deep gratitude to Cackie Upchurch, associate director of the Little Rock Scripture Study, for initiating this project and for providing her insightful suggestions and guidance throughout the development of this manuscript. I am also indebted to Fr. Steve Binz, Johnson Mattingly, Lilly Hess, Nancy Lee Walters, and

Judy Hoelzeman of the Little Rock Scripture Study for their reviews and helpful contributions to this work. I thank my colleagues at the Loyola Institute for Ministry for their commitment to collaborative ministry and their attention to growthful group processes and the facilitators and students of the Loyola Institute for Ministry Extension (LIMEX) who continually teach me new dimensions of group facilitation. Finally, I thank my family and friends who have facilitated my growth over the years.

PART A
PRE-WORKSHOP PREPARATION

1
THE ROLE OF GROUP FACILITATOR

WARM-UP EXERCISES

Before reading the session essay, review the questions and assignments presented below and write your responses in the spaces provided.

A. Reflect and Write:

Recall a highly effective or satisfying small-group discussion in which you participated.

1. What did group members do that helped the discussion develop?

2. What did the facilitator of the group do that helped the discussion develop?

3. Based on your experiences, what would you consider to be the most important characteristics or skills of an effective facilitator?

B. Reading assignment

1. Read the essay "The Role of Group Facilitator" found on the following pages. In the margins note any questions, ideas, or feelings you have in response to the text.

2. Read Luke 22:24-27. Reflect on how the image of leadership presented in this passage might relate to the role of a small-group facilitator.

SESSION ESSAY 1
THE ROLE OF GROUP FACILITATOR

SMALL GROUPS IN CHURCH LIFE

Many of us who grew up in the Catholic faith can remember a time when gathering for prayer and Scripture study in small communities was simply not part of our common Catholic experience. While our brothers and sisters in other Christian denominations had developed Bible study groups as part of their ongoing tradition, Catholics experienced the exciting growth of small community faith gatherings only recently, mainly as a post-Vatican II phenomenon.

During the past quarter century the number of small faith communities in various Christian denominations throughout the world has risen dramatically. These groups vary in form from prayer groups to more action-oriented basic Christian communities (known in Latin America as *communidades de base*), but they all share in their revitalizing effect on their members. Small faith communities are creating new ways of experiencing Church, faith, and God's loving presence among us. Clearly, the Spirit is moving anew among all of God's people.

The Church as the People of God

When Pope John XXIII first spoke of calling together an ecumenical council of the Catholic bishops throughout the world, he used an image of opening a window, allowing fresh air to enter the Church. Nothing less than the wind of the Spirit came rushing in, breathing new life into the Body of Christ. The council reawakened our sense of Church as being most essentially a community, the People of God. Writings emerged from the council reminding us of our early Christian roots and urging us to retrieve the most vital elements of Christian life and to shed the nonessentials. The changes expressed in liturgy, language, and images of Church life all reflected the council's basic intent of enkindling faithfulness to our Christian roots in the context of twentieth-century living.

The council's insistence that the Church is the People of God produced many implications for Church life on both a global and local level. A major implication of this image is that the creation of authentic and loving relationships is central to becoming Church. The People of God are formed by their joyful experience of the saving power of God's love, made most visible for us in the life, death, and resurrection of Jesus. Transformed by our relationship with God, we are called to be a sign and sacrament to the world "of intimate union with God, and of the unity of all [human]kind."[1] As Christ revealed to us in human form the nature of God's love, so the People of God are called to reveal, through the power of the Spirit, the quality of relationships characteristic of the kingdom of God. The bonds among those who claim one another as Church should be signs of hope and of solidarity with all the world's people and creatures.

Loving human relationships are windows into God's heart; to be one with God is to be extravagantly loving. Another way of saying this is that God is Love, and we learn who God is by experiencing and entering into authentic, loving relationships. Ideally, then, we can speak of Church as a network of healthy, vibrant, and growthful relationships among a People who are aware of their source, the God of Love. Empowered by this reality, they work toward renewing the face of the earth and realizing the fullness of God's peace and justice. But we are a Pilgrim People, still in formation, still longing for our full maturity in Christ. Imperfect as they might be, our steps along the way should move us continually onward toward community and toward growth in authenticity. We do this, face to face, first in small groups, then in larger gatherings until our growing sense of trust and solidarity with all of our brothers and sisters and fellow creatures breaks through.

The Emergence of Small Groups
in the Post-Vatican II Church

As the images and directions flowing out from the Second Vatican Council are taking hold of our religious imaginations, new forms of "being Church" are emerging. The council's rootedness in Scripture, its emphasis on community, and its call for solidarity in action on behalf of justice have taken shape in the various forms of community development throughout church life. A brief look at some of these small Christian communities shows the diversity of ways in which the Church is being renewed from within.

Prayer Groups. Since the late sixties, Catholic Christians have literally been "at home" with one another, praying in small group settings outside of church buildings. While neighborhood Rosary groups may have been a forerunner of the home prayer group, the number of these groups, with all their diverse forms, has skyrocketed since the council. Leon Cardinal Suenens, reflecting on the growth of prayer groups mostly within the charismatic renewal movement, centers this growth on both the work of the Spirit and on a rediscovery of the meaning of the Eucharist. He suggests that changes in the liturgical life of the Church have led the faithful to move away from "religious individualism" toward the more traditional experience of Christian prayer life in community. Our experience of the Eucharist has also expanded as it has gained its central place in community worship. Suenens writes that in the celebration of Eucharist, the Spirit not only acts upon the gifts of bread and wine but also transforms the gathered community into the Body and Lifeblood of Christ.[2] Prayer groups are thus a natural extension of the Eucharistic gathering of the Church. They are expressions of the Body of Christ in worship.

Faith-Sharing and Bible Study Groups. In the United States a variety of parish programs centered on faith-sharing and biblical reflection have evoked a new awakening of communal life in congregations that were once assemblies of relative strangers. The highly successful RENEW program was one of the earliest approaches widely adopted by many dioceses across the country and was designed to move groups through six seasons of sharing and reflection on various biblical themes. Dioceses participating in RENEW have consistently reported a renewal of community life in their parishes. The Little Rock Scripture Study has developed a much more expansive program, offering a wide variety of resources and courses for Bible study and faith-sharing in groups. With each of these and similar programs, groups of about four to twelve persons meet together weekly for six to twelve sessions to pray and reflect on Scripture and their own life circumstances.

While Bible study groups are usually centered in prayer, they differ in emphasis from prayer groups. Learning and sharing of personal reflections are central to the purpose of studying Scripture and living out its meaning in everyday life. Participants study biblical commentaries or other outside sources to appreciate the contextual meanings of the scriptural passages chosen. In dialogue they share their reflections as well as their personal life experiences in order to connect the insights of Scripture to their life situations.

Ministry Education Groups. Emerging out of Vatican II's affirmation that ministry is rooted in baptism, thousands of lay people around the country have responded to the call for ministry by seeking out opportunities for updating their theological knowledge and developing new skills. The National Institute for Pastoral Life (formerly in Kansas City, Missouri and now at Loyola University of New Orleans), has been a central resource for dioceses endeavoring to meet this challenge of educating the adult Church for ministry. Many dioceses offer ministry education programs lasting several years for those who will serve in various parish and diocesan ministries, and most of these programs involve small group learning and discussion as part of their overall plan.

These ministry education programs tend to involve a variety of theological and skill-oriented courses involving more intensive study than is usually required in parish-based Scripture study groups. Some, like the Loyola University of New Orleans Extension program (LIMEX), offer a master's degree or a certificate for completing the program.

Basic Christian Communities. House churches, also known as basic Christian communities or intentional Christian communities, share much in common with groups gathering for prayer, faith-sharing, and education for ministry, but they go much further in expressing the range of communal activities that comprise Church life. Most involve regular gatherings for communal worship, group reflection on Scripture and the full historical Christian tradition, the sharing of meals and recreation together, and coordinated efforts toward service and social action. While house churches were the basic form of Church in the first few centuries of Christian history, they gave way in the fourth and fifth century to larger gatherings in basilicas and other "official" church structures. In this century, they re-emerged powerfully in Third World countries and have more recently become a growing American and European phenomenon.[3] A unique aspect of basic Christian communities is their emphasis on public action for the transformation of society.

GROUP FACILITATION

Each of these forms of community life in the Church requires a type of leadership that encourages trust, openness, and the growth of authentic relationships. If the Church is to become fully the People of God, then the people must enter into deepening relationship with one another and, in community, with God. The leadership needed is one that can enhance the development of community in gospel values. In most small-group gatherings, what is needed is a "facilitator."

The word "leader" in our common usage often implies a person who stands apart from a group and directs it. The leader's power is "over" the group and group members are seen as "followers." A "facilitator," on the other hand, is a servant of the group, a person there to help the group achieve its purpose. The facilitator "makes easy" the work of the group, and in a well-functioning group, nearly everyone at one time or another takes on a facilitative role. The facilitator, likewise, is a co-participant with others in the group, sharing personal reflections and experiences and modeling what membership in the group means. Rather than being over the group, the facilitator encourages each member to share in the responsibility for maintaining a healthy and growthful group life.

Several other images may help in describing the work of a group facilitator. One description that is often used is that of an *animator*. The facilitator helps to animate the group by helping it plunge into the heart of the matter to be discussed. Groups can become subdued because of members' anxieties about others' expectations or by members' lack of understanding of the subject matter. The facilitator can help bring life to the group by creating clear guidelines on how the group might proceed and by initiating the conversation, either by posing questions or by sharing some initial thoughts on the subject.

Another image that describes the role of facilitator is that of *completor.* The facilitator ensures that healthy group process happens. Usually, participants help to clarify one another's comments and question each other for deeper reflections. In groups where trust has developed, members feel free to challenge one another and call each other to the norms they have established for themselves (such as coming to the session prepared with all of the readings done). But when such interactions do not happen among the members, the facilitator both encourages participants to take more responsibility for the group and models effective interactions by commenting or bringing up the issues that seem to be blocking the growth of the group. In that sense the facilitator *completes* the group process by providing the needed comments that can help the group get back on track if the group members don't do that for themselves.

Another way of describing this same function is by describing the facilitator as a *skilled participant.* The facilitator is a member of the group and enters into the discussion at hand but is also *skilled* at observing the dynamics of the group and in communicating important information about the group life to its members. As other members learn to notice what helps the group to engage in dialogue and what inhibits it, they too become skilled participants and take on more of the facilitative role for the group. The facilitator is thus ready to share that role with those who are also able to "make easy" the work of the group.

The Facilitator's Role in Faith-Sharing Groups

In Christian study groups the purpose of the gathering is usually to help members grow in knowledge and in faithful living of gospel values. This aim involves the whole person—not just head knowledge, but also heart-felt values and lived experience. The group comes together to help one another integrate the Christian Story and its Vision[4] with their own stories and ideals. In an atmosphere of prayerful reflection and sharing, the group works toward deepening their understanding and receptiveness to the call of the gospel message. They are learning their faith, not just learning *about* their faith.

The facilitator of such a group has a dual role. One is to help each member probe the meaning of scriptural or theological texts and make connections that are relevant to his or her life. By posing questions and inviting members to share, interact, and challenge one another, the facilitator helps members in this work of integration. But another role is just as important for the group facilitator. He or she must help members live their stories in the here-and-now. In a faith-sharing group members cannot remain strangers to one another. The way they relate, hold trusted information in confidence, and respond to their own and one another's anxieties and conflicts all embody how they are living out their faith and Christian Vision in the present. The facilitator helps group members become aware of the way they are interacting with one another, calling participants to greater authenticity and respect.

The Ministry of Facilitation

Facilitating faith-sharing and Scripture study groups is truly a ministry that builds up the Body of Christ at the grassroots. As members work to ground their faith life in both the Christian tradition and their own life experiences, the facilitator ministers by enabling members to explore faith issues honestly.

As a ministry facilitation requires not only the development of specific skills in group observation and communications but also a commitment to prayer and preparation for each session. The prayerful spirituality of the facilitator helps sustain a respectful reverence for members of the group and a stance of humility, even when guiding them through periods of conflict. Since faith development is ultimately the work of the Spirit, the facilitator should continually seek the guidance and strength of the Spirit when helping others listen and respond to the Word of God.

SUMMARY

Faith-sharing communities of various forms have multiplied rapidly in the United States and throughout the world during the latter half of the twentieth century. In Catholic circles these groups are partly a response to Vatican Council II's call that the Church take seriously its role of living as the People of God and working toward the reign of God. Empowered and nourished by the Spirit of God, the faithful become a sacrament of hope to the world as they enter into authentic human community and as they live out the gospel values of compassion and justice.

The style of leadership needed to build such faith communities cannot be one based upon dominance or intolerance. Community emerges as persons become free to dialogue with one another in an atmosphere of respect and mutual caring. The leader of such communities is one who helps members take responsibility for their own interactions and is best described as a "facilitator" of the group process. Group facilitators help to animate discussion through their questions and sharing. They empower others to become cofacilitators of the group and model skillful participation as they become coparticipants in the group's life.

REMINDER: Read Luke 22:24-27 and reflect on how the image of leadership in this passage might relate to the role of small-group facilitator.

NOTES

1. *Lumen Gentium: The Dogmatic Constitution on the Church* in Walter M. Abbott, ed. and Joseph M. Gallagher, trans., *The Documents of Vatican II* (New York: American Press, 1966) 15.

2. Leon Cardinal Suenens *A New Pentecost?* (New York: Seabury Press, 1975) 33–36.

3. Bernard Lee and Michael Cowan, *Dangerous Memories: House Churches and our American Story* (Kansas City, Mo.: Sheed and Ward, 1986).

4. Thomas Groome, *Christian Religious Education* (New york: Harper and Row, 1980) 184. Groome uses the term "Christian Story" to encompass all the various ways that the Christian faith tradition has been expressed throughout its history. "Christian Vision" involves the values and ideals for living and action that the Christian Story portrays.

2
GETTING STARTED

WARM-UP EXERCISES

Before reading the session essay, review the questions and assignments presented below and write your responses in the spaces provided.

A. Reflect and Write:

Recall a time when you first joined a new group.

1. What were your feelings as you entered the place of your gathering and met new people?

2. What questions or concerns were on your mind as you came into the group?

   3. What helped you to feel at ease and at home?

B. Reading assignment

   1. Read the essay "Getting Started" found on the following pages. In the margins, note any questions, ideas, or feelings you have in response to the text.

   2. Read Ephesians 2:12-22 and reflect on your own experiences of growth in Christian community.

SESSION ESSAY 2
GETTING STARTED

Imagine yourself walking into a roomful of people whom you have never previously met. How do you feel? What are your first reactions and approaches? What helps you feel at ease and what increases tension for you?

When I first enter a place where I know few or none of the people, my intuitive and feeling antennas are out sensing the emotional climate of the room. I notice facial expressions and body language and feel more relaxed when I sense warmth, see a smiling face, or hear a welcoming comment. My initial attempts at conversation are usually directed toward finding some common ground or interests through which I can connect with my new-found companions.

For many members of new study groups, their initial session involves meeting a group of people for the first time and entering into a learning and sharing process that they may have never experienced before. As with other situations involving unknowns, the newness of the setting, people, and circumstances may evoke some anxiety or feelings of social awkwardness. One of the facilitator's key tasks in beginning groups is therefore to help create a social climate that enables participants to feel at ease and free to be themselves.

A facilitator can help new members become relaxed with one another and the study process in many ways. Most of these come under the heading of gracious hospitality, a quality highly valued by early Christian communities. Other facilitative approaches are related to ways in which the initial session itself can be structured to create clarity and ease for group members. This chapter is devoted to exploring the importance of good beginnings for Christian small groups and the ways in which those beginnings can be facilitated.

GROUP ISSUES IN THE EARLY STAGES OF GROUP LIFE

Psychologists and others who study groups and group process tend to agree that the initial stages of group formation bring out some common concerns among those who are forming the group. One set of concerns centers on the issue of inclusion—who will be included and to what extent will they be part of this group? Some members may be hesitant and unsure if they really want to join or become an integral member. They may prefer to stay on the edges of the group and watch for a while until they decide. Others may want to be included fully in the group and have a heightened sensitivity to signs of acceptance or rejection by other group members. These members may check some of their spontaneity and ease in order to avoid saying or doing what might be considered the "wrong" thing. For most new members initial sessions are times for "testing the waters" and finding out what norms for group interaction will emerge.

To the extent that participants are unsure about what to expect, regarding either responses from others in the group or the format and depth of discussion that will develop, members will tend to be visibly dependent on the facilitator of the group for guidance and direction. While later in the group's life, participants may readily direct questions to anyone in the group, in the early sessions members tend to direct questions almost exclusively to the facilitator. A mature and developed group will have participants who share the responsibility for bringing up issues important to group process, with participants freely interacting with one another. In early stages of group life, participants will generally wait for the facilitator to take the lead.

The facilitator has several means available for helping a group come together and bond smoothly. One is to create a social climate and opportunities for members to get to know one another. For the group to "gel," the participants need to include one another in their awareness of group life together. One crucial step toward this end is knowing who those others are. Another key task for the facilitator is to provide enough information about the purpose of the gathering and the expectations of group membership to clarify the "unknowns" for participants and to begin naming and developing norms for group interaction that all members can own. Some of those named expectations will offer clarification as to what the facilitator's role is and is not in the group and will help participants form some initial images of what a mature group might look like as it develops over time.

BEFORE THE GATHERING

The Setting

Creating a pleasant setting for group discussion in which group members can feel comfortable and connected with one another goes a long way in helping new members feel at ease in a beginning group. The discussion area should be prepared so that each member has a seat within the circle that is formed. Having some members, especially late-comers, sit outside of the circle creates a symbolic exclusion at a point in the group's life when inclusion is a key issue. Group members should be able to see everyone else in the group easily from each seating position. If chairs are placed around a table, they should be arranged to maximize the visual field of group members. For example, using a long conference table or rectangular table often means that persons seated along the sides cannot easily see the persons immediately to their left or right, and others on the same side of the table may be completely blocked from view. Shorter tables arranged into a hexagon or octagon configuration would create a better visual field for participants. Many times, simply arranging seats in a circle without the table is a preferable option. Regardless of which option is chosen, the important point to keep in mind is that participants need to see each other in a group discussion in order to relate to everyone there as a comember of the group.

Another aspect of the setting that facilitators should attend to in advance is proper lighting. Participants checking their notes or reading assignments should not have to strain for lack of light, nor should they be disturbed by harsh or glaring lights. If a group is meeting in a home, lighting may be unevenly distributed in a room lit by lamps. A little advanced planning can help to minimize distractions in the discussion evoked by deficiencies in the setting.

If videotapes will be used in the session, check that the video equipment is connected properly and working. The tape to be used should be cued to the point where viewing will start, so that the facilitator need not spend time in the session trying to find the location of the evening's videotape lesson. Any other materials needed for the session, such as Bibles, song sheets, newsprint, markers, or handouts should be gathered and placed in a handy location. The setting for shared prayer should also be arranged in advance.

Group members often get to know one another in different ways during break times than they do during discussion time. Having refreshments available enhances the socializing that naturally occurs during breaks. The facilitator can bring the refreshments for the first meeting and then ask volunteers to bring refreshments for subsequent meetings if the group chooses to do so.

The People

Beginning groups should generally start with no more than twelve to fifteen persons.[1] Larger groups create difficulties in involving everyone in the discussion and in enabling members to get to know one another. Groups with less than five persons may dwindle through attrition to a size too small to continue. The program coordinator can assist the facilitator in ensuring a complete list of participants for the study group.

Some groups form from natural circles of friends or church committees so that most members know at least one other person in the group. Nevertheless, becoming part of a Scripture study or faith-sharing group may be a new endeavor for many in the beginning group, and newcomers may have many questions about what to expect. The facilitator can help to create a sense of ease among new members by calling each person who has expressed an interest in joining the group before the first session. The phone conversation can include the facilitator's expression of welcome to the new group member, a brief description of what the study sessions will be like, some mention of who will be joining the group, and an offer to answer any questions the new member may have.

The facilitator can also use the list of participants to create name tags for each person coming to the first session. While name tags may not be necessary at every meeting, they will help participants learn each other's names without having to ask one another repeatedly throughout the acquaintance process. Having name tags prepared ahead of time will free the facilitator to greet and introduce people as they arrive. Keeping some blank tags available is a good idea, too, in case an unannounced participant decides to join the group at the last minute or a person prefers using a nickname.

THE FIRST SESSION

As groups form, they develop norms or general expectations and guidelines that members are expected to follow. Usually, the norms are the ground rules that help group members interact smoothly and stay on task with their primary purpose. However, subtle and unspoken norms can also develop that take the group away from its purpose and prevent healthy communications. A group, for example, can get into the habit of socializing for the first twenty or thirty minutes of meeting time, so that the norm becomes one of always starting the meeting late. If a pattern develops that only three or four of the members do the talking while others listen, it may become the expected pattern—a norm. Like habits, the norms that develop early in a group's life tend to be relatively enduring and difficult to change later on. Thus, the facilitator from the start needs to help the group develop healthy norms and clarify expectations that will enhance the group's work. This process is a gentle one and involves identifying the spirit in which the group might work together rather than "laying down the law."

Shared Prayer

As Thomas Groome reminds us, growth in spiritual development and in the capacity to live out one's faith is a grace of God and requires particular attention to the activity of prayer.[2] Similarly, developing a vibrant Christian community is ultimately the work of the Spirit of God in and through us. Times of shared prayer when group members focus upon and open themselves to the presence of the Spirit are of immeasurable value to the growth of true Christian community. The facilitator's attention to creating an inviting atmosphere conducive to prayer is essential, especially in the formative meetings of the group's life.

Each of the Little Rock Scripture Study sessions begins with a time of prayer for the large group. If some group members are participating in the community prayer by reading or leading some part of the service, they should know where their parts occur within the overall plan. Each small group is encouraged to use conversational prayer as part of their sharing time. For some, this may be a new experience. The facilitator can anticipate participants' possible questions about what is expected of them by describing briefly what the shared prayer will include before beginning. By giving members enough information, the facilitator enables participants to enter more freely into the prayer at a pace that is comfortable for each person.

Introductions

Even when members of a new group know one another from other settings, they often know each other to varying degrees. Beginning the first session with an introduction of each person gives members time to focus on each participant as a fellow member of *this* group and initiates the development of group identity.[3] The structure for the introductions also provides a non-threatening way for encouraging each member in the group to speak to the others. Since it is a participative and inclusive activity, no one assumes the role of spectator.

When structuring the introduction process, the facilitator might make the exercise more interesting by asking members to share something about themselves besides their name and occupation (or parish membership). For example, the facilitator might invite participants to share their favorite story or passage from the Bible or to say something about why they chose to join in Scripture study at this time. Sharing should be brief. Thus, in giving the directions for introductions, the facilitator should clearly state the expectation that each person make concise comments or limit their sharing to one or two minutes. By going first the facilitator can also model the length and type of introduction for the others. The process need not go systematically around the circle of participants. Instead, participants might introduce themselves in any order they choose. The facilitator should suggest the general procedure for introductions before starting.

Explaining the Program

At the start of a new study program, the facilitator should go over the format and materials of the program with the participants, answering any questions the group members might have. The purpose of each component of the program (such as the commentary material and study questions) should be thoroughly explained, even when the majority of the group has met together previously. Since the facilitator knows what the format and expectations of the program are, he or she has the initial responsibility of communicating the basic expectations to the members. With full information, they in turn will be able to share in the responsibility of maintaining a well functioning group.

Eye Contact: A Sign of Inclusion

One powerful sign of inclusion in a group is making eye contact at some point with the person who is speaking. If a group member only looks at one or two other persons to the exclusion of the others, he or she is drawing lines, perhaps unconsciously, indicating who is "in" and who is "out" of the group. The facilitator, especially, should be careful when speaking to make eye contact with all members of the group and should also encourage others to do the same.

Group Agreement

Rather than leaving the formation of group norms to chance or to haphazard formation, many learning and faith-sharing groups review and agree to an explicit set of norms that they intend to work toward in their interactions with one another. While the agreement does not present hard and fast rules, it does openly state the basic norms that will help the group accomplish its purpose. Developing the agreed upon set of norms might be as simple as suggesting some ground rules that participants follow and asking for consensus from the group. Often, the basic norms are set in writing so that the group can refer back to the written agreement from time to time.

Some groups create a list of statements that begin with "I will . . . ." and ask each member to amend and sign the agreement. Others simply present a list of do's and don'ts. The wording is not as important as the content—a basic set of actions that members will strive for so that the group can achieve its goals and communicate effectively. Group members should also be given an opportunity to add to the list or delete or amend any statements that seem troublesome to them. Since ownership of the norms by group members is important to their use in the group, ample time should be allowed for participants' responses and discussion of the proposed agreement. A sample learning agreement is presented at the end of this essay. It can be duplicated for use with new groups.

It is often useful to ask participants to bring their group agreement with them to each session so that they can periodically reflect on it. In assessing their interactions in light of the agreement, group members might note the progress they are making in specific areas and also see where further adjustments and growth need to be made.

SUMMARY

Beginnings are important to the success of any endeavor and are especially important to the development of a healthy group life. Participants joining a new Scripture study or faith-sharing group often face many unknowns—new people, new processes, new challenges. As with other unknowns, the unfamiliar situation of forming a study group can raise some initial anxieties that need to be addressed so that members can be free to be themselves and communicate honestly with one another. Participants need clear information on what to expect in their study group and what is expected of them.

While members will ordinarily grow in the amount of responsibility they assume for healthy group functioning, the tendency in new groups is for participants to rely heavily on the facilitator for leadership and direction. The facilitator's key role during the formation of a group is to help members get to know one another and to establish clear and comfortable norms for their group interactions, enabling them to eventually cofacilitate the group process. The facilitator also helps to set the tone for the group's work together through hospitality, enthusiasm, prayerfulness, and clarification of expectations.

REMINDER: Read Ephesians 2:12-22 and reflect on your own experiences of growth in Christian community.

NOTES

1. The Little Rock Scripture Study recommends no more than twelve participants per group. Other programs have slightly higher limits.

2. Thomas Groome, *Christian Religious Education* (San Francisco: Harper & Row, 1980) 75.

3. Introductions are important, even when only one new person is joining an existing group. Chapter 8 discusses the inclusion of new members into an existing group more fully.

GROUP AGREEMENT

As a gift to others and to myself in this group, I will share in the responsibility of maintaining a prayerful and vibrant Scripture study group. Specifically, I will do my best to live the following guidelines in participating in this group:

1. I will come prepared to Scripture study sessions, having completed the reading and study assignments.

2. I will not miss sessions, except for emergencies, since the life of the group depends on each of us being present to one another.

3. I will share who I am with others, expressing my thoughts, opinions, and feelings honestly with others in the group.

4. I will listen to others without trying to give advice; I will respect differences of opinions without insisting that others agree with my position.

5. I will maintain the confidentiality of the group; I will not repeat outside of this group the personal information I hear within this group.

6. I will encourage others to go deeper in their understanding of Scripture; I will support them in their searching.

7. I will help to make sure that everyone who wants to speak has an opportunity to speak within the group.

_____   _____

Signature   Date

3
COMMUNICATION BASICS—
EXPRESSIVE SKILLS

WARM-UP EXERCISES

Before reading the session essay, review the questions and assignments presented below and write your responses in the spaces provided.

A. Reflect and Write:

Recall a small-group discussion in which you participated.

1. Did any members express their ideas and feelings so that others felt invited to comment even with differing views? How did they do this?

2. Did any members express their ideas or views in a way that seemed to inhibit disagreement or further discussion? How did they do this?

B. Reading assignment

1. Read the essay "Communication Basics—Expressive Skills" found on the following pages. In the margins note any questions, ideas, or feelings you have in response to the text.

2. Read Jeremiah 1:4-10. Consider what your current strengths and weaknesses in expressing your thoughts and feelings are.

SESSION ESSAY 3
COMMUNICATION BASICS—EXPRESSIVE SKILLS

THE IMPORTANCE OF COMMUNICATION

As the People of God we are called to form relationships that reveal the reign of God. In our families, in our workplaces and neighborhoods, and especially in our faith communities, the bonds we form with one another should reflect the bond of Christ with his Church. These relationships are forged and expressed through our interactions with one another, and their quality depends largely on our ability to communicate skillfully and respectfully.

It is no accident that the words "community," "communion," and "communication" all sound somewhat alike. They share common roots and spring from the Latin words *cum* ("with") and *unus* ("one"). All involve some form of being "one with" another. Communion denotes the most profound level of being one with another. Two become one as in marriage, or the many become one Body as in the communion of the faithful in the Eucharist. Community is an expression of being one with others where unity is felt and enjoyed. A sense of oneness on some central values or beliefs connects those in who are in community. Communication also involves a sense of being present to one another as bridges of understanding are built. At the most basic level, community and communion are the fruit of healthy and respectful communications.

Since the quality and character of our relationships are shaped by the ways in which we communicate, a significant part of the facilitator's work in a Scripture study or faith-sharing group is fostering communication styles that express respect and encourage trust among members. The facilitator initially does this by modeling skillful communication in both listening and speaking. As a coparticipant in the group, the facilitator can provide examples of healthy communication styles. The facilitator further assists others to sharpen their own communication skills by intervening in discussions and helping members either express more clearly what they are trying to say or deepen their understandings of what others are expressing. An effective facilitator (and a skilled participant) always listens to what is happening to a group on two levels. On one level, the facilitator is attending to the topic at hand and participating fully in the conversation, and on the other, the facilitator is listening to *how* ideas and feelings are being communicated and assisting group members wherever necessary to communicate more clearly and constructively.

This chapter and the next present brief descriptions of some of the key skills and principles of effective communications that all members of the group can use to maintain an atmosphere of trust and respect in sharing. This chapter offers a presentation of the *expressive* skills, those that enable participants to voice their ideas and feelings in ways that are clear, respectful, and facilitative of ongoing dialogue. The next chapter focuses on effective listening skills.

EXPRESSIVE SKILLS

Congruence

Expression of ideas and feelings involves more than just words. Our gestures, facial expressions, eye movements, and voice tones all convey information about what we are thinking and feeling. For example, facial expressions can reveal if we are convinced or puzzled about a statement or if we are agreeing or disagreeing with what is being said. Some communication experts estimate that up to 85 percent of our personal expressions are non-verbal rather than verbal. Our body language speaks louder than our words, and if our words do not match what our body language is saying, more often than not, people will believe the non-verbal messages and doubt the words. When our words and body language don't match, we are giving a mixed message or one that is incongruent. For example, a speaker could say in a very low, monotone voice, "I am very excited and happy to be here," and we might wonder why her words of excitement don't match her manner and tone of voice. The message is mixed because one channel of expression, voice tone, gives a different message than the other channel, her words. A friend may bellow out, "I'm not angry!" while pounding his fist on a desk. We are likely to question his words since all his gestures and voice give clues of some presence of anger.

A congruent message is one in which all of our expressions, verbal and non-verbal, are communicating the same message. We are not saying one thing and doing another. Congruence implies an awareness not only of my thoughts but of my feelings and an ability to describe both to others. Since incongruent messages are often confusing to those who receive them, they can affect the level of trust in a group if left unchecked.

A facilitator of a group can help members communicate congruently with one another first by becoming aware of his or her own emotions as they occur. By naming some of those emotions in the context of the discussion, the facilitator helps group members tune into their own feelings and deepen their own self-awareness. In commenting on scriptural passages, for example, a facilitator might say, "I felt surprised when I read . . . ." or "I felt comforted by verse 27. . . ." Including emotions as well as opinions and interpretations in the conversation helps members bring their whole selves and not just their intellects into the study of Scripture.

When someone expresses a feeling in a way that seems to be incongruent, the facilitator or another member might check the meaning of the speaker's message by reflecting back to the speaker what is being observed. For example, the facilitator might say something like, "You said you were happy when you read that passage, but I seem to hear a note of sadness in your voice." The speaker is then free to explore or affirm the earlier statement. Notice that the observations are stated as observations and not as conclusions, such as "You said you were happy but you really are sad." To make such an assertion would imply that my observations of the person are more valid than his or her own. Such an imposed interpretation, which goes beyond the few observations I have, can often be heard as a sign of disrespect.

Lack of congruence may never emerge in a group as an issue. If everyone feels free to express their ideas and feelings and does so congruently without any help, the group is well on its way to bonding into a community of faith and caring. But if one or more members tend to communicate incongruently, the trust level in the entire group may suffer. Helping the group establish an atmosphere where true feelings can be expressed freely rather than denied is an important function for the entire group and especially for the facilitator.

Using "I" Language

Clear verbal messages consist of words that match the reality that they are expressing. We have explored one sign of matching, congruence, in which one's verbal and non-verbal signals are all sending the same message. Another area of communication where matching is needed involves how we each express "ownership" of our perceptions, thoughts, and emotions. Our expressions of opinion should match the reality of our limited and unique perspectives.

Each of us has a distinct point of view on the world around us and the situations we encounter. We bring to the present moment all of our past history and our future hopes and dreams, and these color what we notice in a situation and what words and events mean to us. No two people see the same event or hear a message in exactly the same way. The thoughts and reactions that are triggered, the memories that are evoked all differ with our unique personalities and conditioning.

Clear communication involves stating my thoughts and perceptions in a way that acknowledges that they spring from my own unique perspective, even though that perspective is largely shaped by the culture and influence of others. I can only tell you what I have observed, what I think, and what I feel. You may see the situation differently or experience different reactions than I do. If I were to say, for example, "Everybody hates rainy days," I am expressing my own reaction without acknowledging that someone else may have a different response. What's more, I have stated my preference as a statement of *fact*. Now someone who disagrees is put in a position of challenging my statement of fact rather than of simply offering a different response. While this is a rather uncomplicated example, it provides an illustration of the type of language that can strain discussions involving deeper levels of values and commitments.

The use of "I" language clearly states the source of perceptions and opinions and leaves room for others to have differing viewpoints. Basically, "I" language consists of expressing my ideas and feelings by beginning the message with the word "I." For example, "I think that Paul in this passage is saying . . . ." or "I believe that . . . ." or "I feel. . . ." The message is clearer because it matches the reality of the situation—when I state an opinion, I am expressing my own unique perspective and not a universal "fact."

When reporting to others one's own observations of their behavior, the use of "I" language is extremely important to communicating clearly and minimizing defensiveness on the part of the listener. Beginning feedback statements with "you" language tends to be interpreted easily as a statement of blame, especially if used in conjunction with broad labels rather than specific descriptions of behavior. (For example, a statement such as "You are dominating the discussion" will almost assuredly evoke defensiveness on the part of the listener.) An "I" language statement clearly reports the information as a personal perception and not as an undeniable fact. (An example would be something like, "I feel somewhat anxious when you give so much detail about your stories because I am aware of our limited time for discussion.") Using I-statements to report observations enables me to be honest while respecting the uniqueness of the person to whom I am speaking.

The word respect comes from the Latin word *respicere*—to behold. When I communicate respectfully, I am basically beholding the other as someone separate and different from myself. I do not assume that my opinions are the "right" ones or that my feelings are universally felt. In dialogue I bring forth my viewpoints and reactions and make room for the other person to do the same. By using I-statements I acknowledge that we are each unique, and I allow the other person to state a different point of view.

Concreteness

Concreteness refers to expressing observations and ideas in specific rather than in general terms. When I am concrete in describing my experiences, I describe situations giving some information about what happened, when it happened, and what I was specifically thinking or feeling at the time. This skill is especially important in relating Scripture to life experiences and in giving feedback to another person about what I am observing. Let's look at two examples.

Example A: "When I read the Beatitudes in Matthew's Gospel (5:1-12), I felt good. I heard that God loves us and can turn our pain and suffering around, even if we don't see a way that it can happen. I have had some life experiences that confirm this."

Example B: "When I read in Matthew's Gospel, 'Blessed are those who are persecuted for righteousness' sake" (5:10), I remembered a time when I became friends with and cared for a neighbor who had AIDS, even though others in the neighborhood began criticizing me. Somehow I knew that I was living a gospel message and I had a growing sense of joy, even in my discomfort with the conflicts."

While these examples are relatively short, they illustrate some differences in concreteness. Example A is expressed in very general terms. There are no specific examples or situations described. The feeling statement that is presented is also very vague ("I felt good") rather than offering some specific information ("I felt comforted" or "hopeful"). While Example B does not present many details, it does give some specific (concrete) information about the life experience that the person is retrieving.

Communicating in concrete terms enables us to share more of ourselves with others and keeps us grounded in the everyday reality of our lives. Without concreteness in our communications, our expressions remain vague and abstract. In giving others feedback that they can use, the skill of concreteness is extremely important. For example, if I say, "You did a nice job tonight in our discussion," the person I am speaking to might feel flattered but would know little about what I was talking about. If instead I said, "I appreciated the way you asked me questions about what I meant by 'covenant'; they helped me clarify my own thinking," then I have given some specific information about what I found helpful. To be helpful, feedback to others should be *specific* in describing the behaviors that are perceived to be helpful and those that seem to be hindering the dialogue in the group.

Appropriate Self-Disclosure

Most discussion groups will experience a broad range of participant sharing styles. Some participants have little to say and often speak toward the end of the meeting if at all. Others have so much to share that the entire session could be devoted to listening to their issues. While the time in a faith-sharing group does not need to be equally apportioned among all participants, it should be distributed so that all are invited to have some say or sharing in the discussion.

A well-functioning group generally develops a norm of appropriate levels of self-disclosure among members in their discussions. While it may not be explicitly stated, the norm guides members to share details only to the extent that they are pertinent to the discussion at hand. When a story or statement becomes so laden with particulars that the threads of the story get lost, this norm has been breached and other members of the group may start squirming. If over-sharing of details seems to be a possible problem in the group, the facilitator might suggest an explicit norm asking that members help ensure that everyone has a chance to participate in the discussion.

SUMMARY

Communication lies at the heart of dialogue and forms the basis for all community-building. In faith-sharing and Scripture study groups, healthy communication provides the key to group growth in trust and depth of sharing. While effective communication begins with the desire to open up and reach another person, its realization requires the development of skills in both expressing ideas and feelings and in listening to others.

Expressive skills hinge upon a basic level of self-awareness. Even if we are unaware of our feelings, we often express them anyway through our body language and non-verbal signals. A person who is aware and honest about what he or she is expressing will be able to give a congruent message, a verbal message that matches the non-verbal expressions of feeling and thought.

The use of I-statements is also an essential component of respectful and honest communications. When I own my thoughts and feelings through "I" language, I responsibly express my opinions and leave room for others either to agree or disagree. Concrete expressions that describe my specific, lived experiences allow others to get to know me and provide helpful information to others in the form of feedback. Finally, these expressions need to be limited in the amount of detail they provide so that my level of sharing is appropriate in self-disclosure to the topic at hand.

REMINDER: Read Jeremiah 1:4-10 and reflect upon your current strengths and weaknesses in expressing your thoughts and feelings.

4
COMMUNICATION BASICS—
LISTENING SKILLS

WARM-UP EXERCISES

Before reading the session essay, review the questions and assignments presented below and write your responses in the spaces provided.

A. Reflect and Write:

1. Recall a group experience in which you felt truly listened to and understood. What did others do to let you know that they were listening to you and understanding?

2. Read Acts 15:1-22. Reflect on the image of listening that occurred at the Council of Jerusalem as Barnabas and Paul described their work among the Gentiles to those present.

   a. What kind of scene do you imagine?

b. How does the scene you imagined compare to your experience of meetings in which there has been a heated debate on an important issue?

B. Reading assignment

1. Read the essay "Communication Basics—Listening Skills" found on the following pages. In the margins note any questions, ideas, or feelings you have in response to the text.

SESSION ESSAY 4
COMMUNICATION BASICS—LISTENING SKILLS

If persons in faith-sharing groups are joining together as Church community, then as Paul Ripple[1] and others tell us, they are called to be friends. Bernard Cooke, in his book *Sacraments and Sacramentality,* reminds us that true friendships give us a glimpse of God's love for us.[2] Similarly, the Book of Sirach tells us that a faithful friend is a "sturdy shelter . . . a treasure beyond price" (6:14-15). Friends are those who give us life, those with whom we can freely share the thoughts of our heart. Friends listen to one another, even through the silent spaces between spoken words, and they understand.

Perhaps nothing is more essential to the development of friendship than the ability to listen with a depth of understanding. The gift of listening is truly a life source, and it brings out the best and most human in each of us. Therapist Carl Rogers and consultant Richard Farson write that skillful, "active" listening is the primary catalyst for both individual and group growth:

> Listening brings about changes in people's attitudes toward themselves and others, and also brings about changes in their basic values and personal philosophy. People who have been listened to in this new and special way become more emotionally mature, more open to their experiences, less defensive, more democratic, and less authoritarian.
>
> When people are listened to sensitively, they tend to listen to themselves with more care and make clear exactly what they are feeling and thinking. Group members tend to listen more to each other, become less argumentative, more ready to incorporate other points of view.[3]

Active listening is a set of skills and an art whereby the listener both assists the speaker in expressing the fullness of his or her ideas and feelings and also communicates an understanding of the speaker's whole message. This approach to listening requires respect for the person who is speaking. It also involves a willingness to explore the person's message on its own terms, regardless of how different from one's own or how personally challenging it might be. The listener's initial responses are not rebuttals nor reactions but are reflections of the speaker's own communications, often with invitations to say more.

THE NON-VERBALS OF LISTENING

Good listening begins with attention. The listener sets aside the "internal dialogue" of daydreams and personal planning to focus attention entirely on the speaker. This kind of concentration requires that we refrain from taking "mental vacations" from the conversation. Instead, we listen with wholehearted openness to what the speaker is communicating, both in words and in non-verbal expressions.

Our own posture and non-verbal actions can help us focus on a speaker or can deflect our attention away from the other person. If, for example, I am looking around the room as someone else is speaking, my visual attention is focused away from the speaker, and my visual field will soon compete with my hearing of the speaker's words. I will also fail to notice the gestures and facial expressions that accompany those words. If I sit in such a slouched position that my body feels that it's almost nap time, my alertness and attention will be affected. If I fidget with small objects or leaf through pages of a book as a person is talking, I again divide my attention. Within the interaction itself, my actions may be so distracting that the speaker can begin to focus on my activity and lose track of his or her own train of thought.

Our attention to another person in conversation should be reflected in our non-verbal behavior. The listener's posture should be relaxed and facing the speaker, not angled away. Eye contact is important and is usually frequent between speaker and listener. Activities not related to listening should be set aside. In short, all of our non-verbal behaviors should communicate a receptive and attentive listening stance toward the speaker. Like a sacrament, our non-verbal actions both signify our attentiveness and participate in that reality.

ACTIVE LISTENING SKILLS

One major block to effective communication is the tendency to take understanding for granted, both on the part of the listener and on the part of the speaker. I may give directions to someone and watch the person nod in apparent comprehension. I may even ask, "Did you understand everything I said?" and receive a firm response of "yes." Then, I watch in utter amazement as the person drives away in the opposite direction I just mapped out.

As a listener I may be convinced that I understand the feelings and opinions that another person is expressing, only to find out later that I was mistaken. The practice of active listening helps us to avoid these misunderstandings. It requires that we check periodically with the person who is speaking to verify our understanding of his or her message.

The main purpose of active listening is to assist the speaker in expressing clear and complete messages, and the active listener does this in several ways. One way is by encouraging the speaker to continue by simply responding to what is being said without changing the subject. A second way that the active listener supports the speaker is by "reflecting back" to the speaker the content, both explicit and implied, that has been expressed. The speaker is then able to hear what he or she has said in a new light. Active listeners support the speaker in a third way by inviting the speaker to say more about the topic. In a sense the active listener draws the speaker out by posing questions that the speaker may not have yet considered or by inviting the speaker to focus more clearly on one or more aspects of the subject. Composing questions, as is explored in the next chapter, is an art especially central to the work of group facilitation.

Some of the active listening skills are second-nature to us because of the many times we use them in our daily conversations. Others may seem foreign or awkward to us because they have rarely been part of our conversational repertoire. We tend to develop habitual patterns of communicating and may tend to avoid changes that break our habits. But it is precisely in changing our habits that we grow in the art of listening.

Skill development exercises help us to discover our conversational habits, both good and bad. They enable us to learn new skills that can be practiced and interwoven into our existing communication patterns. The challenge to us is often to persevere in practicing the new skills until they become comfortably owned and integrated into our personal styles.

I invite you to explore which of the active listening skills presented here seem somewhat different from your current habits and to take these up as a challenge. Practice these skills until they flow naturally, and then decide if they are usable to you at various times in your conversations and facilitation.

Skill 1: Reflecting Explicit Content

A basic skill in active listening is the ability to reflect or paraphrase accurately the content of another person's message. If I cannot repeat back what the other person has said, I was probably not paying attention while the person was speaking, or I distorted what I heard because of my own needs, conditioning, or perceptions. Reflecting back content periodically enables us to check our own assumptions of understanding and lets the speaker know that we are following his or her line of thought.

This skill mainly involves simply paraphrasing or saying what the speaker has said in our own words. Sometimes, if the speaker is going breathlessly on with a message or story, we may need to break in with a statement such as, "Let me see if I understand you correctly. . . ." and then follow with our paraphrased version of what we have heard. Some examples of paraphrased statements are provided below:

Example 1:

SPEAKER: When I drive to work, I pass a street that has a soup kitchen and homeless shelter. So many people are always standing there in line. It bothers me that this problem is growing, and I simply pass by every day.

LISTENER: You are bothered by your lack of response to so many people in need?

Example 2:

SPEAKER: I always heard that the Bible was the Word of God and is true. Now I hear that the story of creation in the Book of Genesis is just that—a story. I don't see how we can speak of the truth of Genesis if what it says about Adam and Eve is a story.

LISTENER: What you have always heard about truth and the Bible, particularly regarding the story of creation in Genesis, is different from what you are hearing now?

Notice that in these examples the information that is reflected back to the speaker stays close to what he or she actually said. The paraphrase simply and briefly states the content that is being heard, and the speaker is given back the "air time" to continue speaking and elaborating.

Skill 2: Reflecting Underlying Feelings

Rogers and Farson contend that in many cases the content of a message is far less important to the total meaning than the feelings which underlie the content.[4] Emotions color our words and point to the deeper levels of significance that we attach to our experiences. In active listening, paraphrasing helps the speaker get the story out. Reflecting the underlying feelings helps the speaker attend to the deeper levels of meaning that the story holds.

To reflect back the underlying feelings accompanying a message, the listener needs to observe not only the spoken words but also the many non-verbal cues and modes of expression that the speaker is using. We need to listen between the lines of what is being said to offer some accurate reflections of feeling back to the speaker. Let's go back to the two examples we presented earlier.

Example 1:

SPEAKER: When I drive to work, I pass a street that has a soup kitchen and homeless shelter. So many people are always standing there in line. It bothers me that this problem is growing, and I simply pass by every day.

LISTENER: You feel saddened by their plight and also feel a desire to do something?

Example 2:

SPEAKER: I always heard that the Bible was the Word of God and is true. Now I hear that the story of creation in the Book of Genesis is just that—a story. I don't see how we can speak of the truth of Genesis if what it says about Adam and Eve is a story.

LISTENER: You're feeling confused and upset by the mixed messages you are receiving on this?

In both examples the questioning tone of the listener's response allows the speaker to correct any misperceptions that may exist. The focus on feelings moves the speaker away from the details of the actual experience to an exploration of the personal meaning of that experience. The art of active listening involves sensing when to help the speaker explore and describe the experience further and when to move to deeper personal reflections.

Skill 3: Reflecting Implications

An important element of problem-solving is the ability to imagine possible consequences or implications of a decision or course of action. An active listener can use a third type of reflection, that of reflecting back possible implications, to help a speaker consider the full import of a particular stance or conclusion. Usually this form of reflection is used in later stages of an exploration after the person has had ample opportunity to explore experiences and underlying feelings. If used too early, this form of active listening intervention could result in a premature move to problem-solving or decision-making before the topic is thoroughly explored. Some examples:

Example 1:

SPEAKER: I guess I'm just realizing that even though I get a high salary, I don't feel that I'm really contributing to creating a better world. My work feels pretty meaningless and I long to do something that I consider worthwhile.

LISTENER: It sounds as though you may be considering a job change to work that is more meaningful to you, even though it may not pay as well as your current job?

Example 2:

SPEAKER: I think what Paul is basically saying in this passage (1 Cor 11:17-34) is that the community must first recognize and care for Christ in others if they are going to participate in the Lord's Supper.

LISTENER: It sounds as though the Eucharist has many social implications for you.

Reflecting implications is quite different from advice-giving. In this mode of active listening, the listener is still reflecting back the meaning that is emerging from the speaker's message. The listener attempts to bring out consequences or future actions that are implied in what the speaker is saying. Advice-giving usually springs from the advice-giver's own experiences and often deflects speakers away from exploring the meaning of their own situations.

Skill 4: Probing for New Information

In each of the three "reflecting" skills, the listener's statement is either tentatively stated or phrased as a question because the listener is checking that the reflective statement provides an accurate description of what the speaker has said. Most often, the reflective statement is presented in the form of a question. The speaker is thereby invited to correct any inaccuracies.

When we probe for new information, we are not trying to rephrase the speaker's statements or implied messages. Instead, we are inviting the speaker to open up new avenues of description or reflection. The listener's probing in the form of a question or a directive focuses the conversation and asks the speaker to provide new or more in-depth content from what has been previously expressed.

Probing statements can either be *closed-ended* or *open-ended*. When questions are highly structured and allow for only 'yes' or 'no' responses or other one-word answers, they are often referred to as *closed-ended*. When questions are stated to allow the speaker the freedom to develop the response in his or her own personal style, they generally are called *open-ended*.

Directives, too, probe for new information. They are stated in the form of imperatives rather than questions (e.g., "Tell me more about your family") and can also either be closed-ended or open-ended, depending upon their wording.

Closed-ended questions and directives are often used on surveys or questionnaires, but they tend to be limiting or constraining if used exclusively in ordinary conversation and discussions. A well-conceived open-ended question creates the spark that initiates a lively discussion and fruitful dialogue. In some cases the two can be used effectively in combination. A brief closed-ended question might help to focus on a particular experience, and an open-ended question that followed would evoke reflection. (For example: Have you ever been in a faith sharing group before? What did you like most about that experience?) Some further examples of both closed-ended and open-ended probing statements are listed below.

CLOSED-ENDED QUESTIONS:
    How many children do you have?
    What is your name?
    Where do you work?

OPEN-ENDED QUESTIONS:
    What activities do you enjoy most in your present job?
    Why do you think that is so?
    How do the experiences of Mark's community in this passage
        relate to your own?

CLOSED-ENDED DIRECTIVES:
    Please introduce yourself, stating your name and occupation.
    Tell me which pages you read for homework this week.

OPEN-ENDED DIRECTIVES:
    Please introduce yourself, telling us something about your favorite
        hobbies and leisure activities.
    Tell me more about what this passage meant to you.

Much more can be said about the art of designing questions in relation to facilitating group discussions. The next chapter will address the topic of various types of discussion questions. For now, it is important to note that inviting more information from the speaker is part of active listening and that open-ended probes are usually more effective than closed-ended ones.

ACTIVE LISTENING AND GROUP FACILITATION

Active listening is a set of skills that can be used in one-on-one conversations or in group discussions. The use of these skills by a group facilitator depends largely on the type of group that is formed, its purpose and its norms. For example, in some support and therapy groups, it would be quite appropriate for a facilitator to spend the entire session actively listening to one person and exploring in depth the meanings and feelings that the individual was attaching to an experience. In a discussion group gathered to study and reflect upon Scripture, such in-depth work with one individual would usually be inappropriate. The aim, instead, may be to focus on a passage of Scripture and explore the many ways that the passage touched people's lives, connected with their experiences, and moved them to action. The variety of perspectives of all group members are important to exploring the richness of the text, and active listening on the part of all members should serve that purpose.

The facilitator of a group needs a keen sense of timing. Sometimes, the facilitator's best course of action is allowing the discussion to proceed without intervening. For example, if the group is managing the discussion well and the participants are responding to one another, then the facilitator need not take the role of "reflector" or "questioner" since other group members are providing these functions. Indeed, the facilitator could inadvertently deflect the flow of the conversation and become the center of attention by injecting too many questions or reflective statements at times when they are not needed. The guiding principle to keep in mind is that interventions should "facilitate" the discussion by clarifying and communicating understanding when needed.

SUMMARY

One of the greatest gifts we can give to another is the gift of understanding. It forms the basis of true friendship and lies at the heart of dialogue. One means by which we can reach for deeper levels of understanding and communicate that understanding to others is through active listening.

Active listening is both an art and a set of skills. It begins with a stance of respect, humility, and attention while another is speaking and involves non-verbal as well as verbal behaviors. Our body language, such as eye contact and posture, should be directed to the speaker.

Verbally, active listening requires checking our understanding of what the speaker has said and inviting the speaker to say more. We can check our understanding by (1) reflecting explicit content, (2) reflecting underlying feelings, and (3) reflecting back to the speaker the implications that we have heard or understood. We invite the speaker to say more when we ask questions or use directives that probe for more information. Open-ended questions are generally more evocative of discussion and reflection than are closed-ended questions.

Facilitators need to listen to their own internal cues and questioning to learn useful moments for clarifying information in a discussion. They also need to be careful not to overuse listening interventions in ways that could interrupt an effective flow of dialogue among participants who are already listening well to one another.

NOTES

1. Paula Ripple, *Called to be Friends* (Notre Dame: Ave Maria Press, 1980).

2. Bernard Cooke, *Sacraments and Sacramentality* (Mystic, Conn.: Twenty-third Publications, 1983) 82.

3. Carl R. Rogers and Richard E. Farson, "Active Listening" in David A. Kolb, Irwin M. Rubin, and James M. McIntyre, eds., *Organizational Psychology: A Book of Readings,* 3rd ed. (Englewood Cliffs: Prentice-Hall, 1979) 170.

4. Ibid., 173.

5
CONNECTING SCRIPTURE
WITH LIFE EXPERIENCES

WARM-UP EXERCISES

Before reading the session essay, review the questions and assignments presented below and write your responses in the spaces provided.

A. Reflect and Write:

Recall a highly effective or satisfying small-group discussion in which you participated. How did the phrasing of the discussion and/or follow-up questions contribute to the quality of the discussion?

B. Reading and Reflection Assignment:

1. Read Luke 10:25-37.
   a. Do any particular lines or parts of that passage stand out for you? Which ones?

      b. What meaning do those lines have for you? (Why do they stand out?)

    2. Read the essay "Connecting Scripture with Life Experiences" found on the following pages. In the margins, note any questions, ideas, or feelings you have in response to the text.

C. Question Development Exercise:

After reading the session essay, complete the Question Development Exercise found on pages 71–72.

SESSION ESSAY 5
CONNECTING SCRIPTURE WITH LIFE EXPERIENCES

THE PURPOSE OF SCRIPTURE STUDY

The central purpose of Scripture study groups is to help participants connect the lessons of Scripture with their own life experiences and situations. This connection is vital for an authentic Scripture study that leads to a deepening of faith. Without it, the study remains distant, abstract, and impersonal. A key role for the facilitator, then, is to enable group members to tell their "stories" and connect them with the experiences, insights, lessons, and visions of the scriptural texts they encounter.

LISTENING TO OUR STORIES

The Bible gives us a collection of narratives about God's movement in the lives of people formed together by historical events that shaped their relationships to God and to one another. Scripture tells the history of God's work of salvation as interpreted by various authors within the cultures of their times. Through them, we come to know the God of Moses, of Ruth, and of Jesus as the One who enters into relationship with us and speaks through the events and people of each epoch. God's presence throughout history implies that if we want to hear how God has worked in and through the lives of our ancestors in Scripture, we need to be open to how God is also working in and through our own lives and circumstances.

Dick Westley, in his book *Redemptive Intimacy,*[1] strongly affirms that we find God in our everyday experiences. He tells us that the Bible becomes the Word of God for us when we accept it as faith testimony about the experiences of God's presence in various communities and then relate those experiences to our own. Unless we are able to perceive our own lives as the place where God acts and speaks to us, we will find it difficult to hear God speaking to us through the Scriptures.

Westley writes, "If God is revealing himself to us in our experience, then it is essential for us believers to take the time and have the institutional mechanisms for gathering to share and get in touch with that experience."[2] As experiences are shared and insights into God's revelation are confirmed by many groups in various places and times, they become recognized as the "consensus" of the faithful or the *sensus fidelium.*[3] Because of the importance of discerning God's Word in our life circumstances, Westley writes that "Dialogue, faith sharing, and experience sharing in the name of the Lord are an essential work of the People of God."[4]

We are still growing in our understanding of the implications of God's Word to us, and we gain new insights by continually conversing with—listening and speaking back to—the texts of Scripture. When we do this in community, we hear the full richness of this conversation in many voices. Ultimately, the meaning of God's Word to us unfolds more deeply as it shapes our responses to life and as we live out its call in our own life situations.

LISTENING TO THE TEXTS OF SCRIPTURE

Studying a text of Scripture involves uncovering many layers of meaning. One is the intended message of the inspired author who wrote for a particular audience at a particular time. To delve into this world of meaning, we need to learn about the social realities, the history, and common symbols of both the people in the story and of those to whom it was addressed. Studying biblical commentaries and the work of biblical scholars can help us enter into those worlds so distant from ours in time and culture. When we have discovered the "voice" of the text, we can then bring its images and lessons into the present and discern its significance for our own life circumstances.

One of the main blocks to hearing what the author of a scriptural text is saying is that of taking our understanding of the text for granted. With scriptural texts we have several stumbling blocks that we often do not encounter in face-to-face interactions. The most basic is that we are reading texts that are at least nineteen hundred years old. By basing our interpretations upon the assumptions we make about our twentieth-century world, assumptions that are different from those made by first-century Jewish and Greek communities, we can easily distort or miss original meanings intended by the authors of scriptural texts.

A second block is that the middle-class First World culture from which many of us come creates a different perspective on the biblical texts than the underclass perspective of most of the communities in which the writings developed. In the United States, we have tremendous difficulty fathoming the conditions of Second and Third World nations. Many of us are part of the dominant culture of this country and have never experienced persecution or discrimination as an outcast of society. Yet, when we read Luke's Gospel and many of the other books of the Bible, we are reading texts written for communities who were often impoverished and were generally persecuted and shunned by the dominant cultures of their day. Unless we can learn about the cultural and historical conditions surrounding the writing of the text, we will miss many of the stunning meanings that are imbedded there.

The assumptions we make about our world will color, and in some cases cloud, the meanings that the author of a text intended to convey. In other ways the circumstances and conditions of our own lives will highlight points in the text (a Word in the text for us) that others of different circumstances may not see. In listening to the biblical texts, we need to use both ears—one for listening to the text in its "own voice" and another to listen to the inner workings of our hearts as the text speaks its particular message for us. Biblical commentaries are helpful in relating some of the cultural information and intended meanings of the authors. As new meanings come to light through our study, we still need to listen with our "other" ear to hear what this text is saying to us and to our community in our particular life situation.

Sometimes our own insights and experiences may lead us to question the assumptions that the original author was using. For example, the letter to the Ephesians exhorts slave owners to be kind to their slaves (6:9) but does not question the institution of slavery. In contrast, human experience and reflection on the Christian message

throughout the centuries have led us as Church to deplore slavery
or any relationship that robs another of basic human dignity. Dis-
cernment of God's Word requires listening with a depth and openness of heart as we draw upon all of our experiences and knowledge.

EXPLORING THE PARABLE OF THE GOOD SAMARITAN

If you read the parable of the Good Samaritan in Luke's Gospel,
you will notice that Jesus' parable was given in response to a lawyer's question. Now, we often interpret the word "lawyer" to mean
a professional who is practicing in civil and secular courts. In the
Jewish world of Jesus' day, a lawyer was one who studied the Law
of Moses, the Torah, that guided the people in living out their Covenant with God and with one another. The lawyer was an interpreter
of these religious teachings for the people, a religious expert. By
his own words in response to Jesus' question, the lawyer in the story
states that the central law of the Torah is loving God and loving
neighbor.

In response to the lawyer's question, "And who is my neighbor?"
Jesus responds with the story of a man who was beaten by robbers
as he traveled from Jerusalem to Jericho. The first man who passed
by without stopping was a priest. In Jesus' day priests were those
considered to be descendants of Aaron (Moses' brother and
spokesperson) and were in charge of the ritual sacrifices at the
Temple altar. They performed the purity rituals prescribed by the
Torah. The second who passed by the man was a Levite, considered to be a direct descendant of Moses. Like the lawyer who was
encountering Jesus, the Levites were those who taught and explained
the true meaning of the Torah.

As we all know the story, the one who stopped and took care
of the man was a Samaritan. Historically, Samaritans had a common claim to the Torah with the Jews, since the city-state Samaria
was once the capital of the ten northern tribes of Israel (the Northern Kingdom). Yet, they were considered outcasts by the Jews because of their *ritual impurity* of mixing and intermarrying with
foreigners and because of their *erroneous interpretation* of the Torah.
The hostility and dispute between the Jews and Samaritans was

mainly one of who the true people of the Torah were.[5] From a Jewish perspective the Samaritans were clearly the heretics.

Yet, in Jesus' story it is the Samaritan who fulfills the Law, the Torah. If Jesus were simply giving an example story for his Jewish listeners, he might have made the hero of the story a Jewish person rather than the controversial Samaritan.[6] One level of meaning in this story is that the Law of God is not fulfilled by purity rituals nor by teaching the Torah but only by living compassion. Membership in God's covenanted people is not even assured by being a descendant of Aaron nor of Moses, the leaders of the people at the initiation of the Covenant. The one who fulfilled the demands of the Torah was the one who cared for the injured and penniless, spending his own resources without thought of return. Regardless of his heritage or theological perspective, the Samaritan was portrayed by Jesus as the true exemplar of the Covenant.

Jesus' story shatters the prevailing view in the dominant culture of his time about who is in God's "inner circle" and who is out—who is in the true Covenant with God and who is not. For the Jewish audience of Jesus' time, those closest to the workings of the Temple, such as the priests and Levites, were the holiest. Next were the Law-abiding Jewish folk. Samaritans and Gentiles were not included in the covenanted people of God. Jesus' parable rips through this view of the world and turns it inside out.

Biblical scholar Robert Karris[7] says that this parable is really about who belongs to the Church and was as relevant to the life questions facing Luke's community as it is today. Luke's second book, the Acts of the Apostles, tells us that the question of who could be admitted as a member of the Church was an explosive one in the early Church (15:1-2). Quite possibly, in the oral tradition of Luke's community, the parable of the Good Samaritan was used in gatherings to reflect on the actual issues of Church membership that were facing them—should Gentiles have equal status with Jews as the People of God? As Karris says, "Luke's answer is revolutionary: The person who observes the covenant law of mercy—be he Jew, Samaritan, or Gentile—is a member of God's church."[8]

Keeping in mind the brief commentary presented here, reread the story of the parable of the Good Samaritan (Luke 10:25-37). Then, imagine how you might hear this passage if you were penniless and suffering. How would you view Jesus in this story? Imagine how you might hear this story if you were a first-century Samaritan or Gentile or if you were a newly converted Jewish member of the Christian community. Finally, what questions does it raise for you in your actual life situation? How do you hear it as a *bona fide* member in good standing of your own church? What responses does it call forth from you and your faith community?

THE ART OF ASKING QUESTIONS

A primary function that the facilitator fulfills in a faith-sharing group is to pose questions for group discussion and assist the group in managing its time. Questions that challenge members to integrate the material presented with their own life experiences are important to faith-sharing and should receive more of the group's time and attention than simple questions of information about the story events or points made in the presentation.

The facilitator's main source of discussion questions in the Little Rock Scripture Study is the study guide that participants use as they reflect daily on their reading assignments. These questions offer a wealth of discussion-starter material, but they are only the beginning of a good discussion. During the dialogue, the facilitator will need to create other questions to assist the group in connecting their own particular life situations with the texts. Some understanding of the various types and purposes of discussion questions may therefore be useful to the facilitator.

Elizabeth Flynn and John LaFaso[9] have identified five kinds of questions that are often used in discussions:

1. *Fact:* These typically ask about points made in the story, commentary, or video presentation and help to highlight key points in the text. Examples are: What were the actual words of the text? What question did the lawyer pose to Jesus? To what city was the traveler in the story going? Who was the first person to pass the injured man without stopping?

2. *Concretizing:* The focus of concretizing is to examine related aspects of the present experience, life situation, or actions of participants. It asks for a concrete example such as: What situation in your community is like this? Where in your life has a question like

this come up? Who in your community are usually considered the "pillars" or inner-circle group?

3. *Meaning:* These questions ask for participants' opinions about the meaning of the events, words, or story. Examples are: How would you describe the meaning of the Torah for the Jewish people? Within the context of its time and place, what meaning did the author intend in this text? What did you mean when you said that this text opened up a new world for you?

4. *Balance or Congruence:* These are questions which seek to explore how a new meaning "fits" with or challenges participants' existing attitudes and opinions. Examples are: How does this interpretation fit with your previous beliefs? What do you feel when you hear this interpretation? How does this story challenge your present actions and opinions?

5. *Response:* These call for an examination of our vision for the future and a decision. What decision for action am I called to make? What changes in the way you view other people does this story call for? What does this story imply for our future actions?

Flynn and LaFaso point out that questions of *meaning* and *response* are probably the most important to be addressed in a discussion group but that they need the support and exploration of the other types of questions in order to be answered adequately.[10] Questions of fact point to key elements in the text but do not ask directly for interpretation. As discussion questions, they have only limited value but may be important in clarifying or providing information that was missed. Concretizing questions help to ground the participants' experience of the scriptural text in their own present actions and circumstances. Questions of balance or congruence help to "unpack" the full import and implications of the meaning of a text for the participant's view of life, relationships, and future action. These "test" the students' current understandings in light of the new meanings arising from the biblical text.

Some general guidelines for posing questions to the group are listed below.[11] They offer some additional suggestions about what to include and what to avoid in all types of questions presented to the group.

1. *Ask open-ended questions whenever possible.* With the exception of questions of "fact" that are often quite pointed to specific answers, discussion questions tend to be more effective and generate more dialogue and reflection when they leave the structure of the response open. Closed-ended questions generally ask for a one-word or short-phrase response and do not of themselves invite deeper reflections. Sometimes closed-ended questions may help to focus on a particular experience and are useful if followed immediately with a more open-ended question. For example, if a closed-ended question were posed such as, "Have you ever worked in a soup kitchen before?" it might be followed by an open-ended question such as, "What was that experience like for you?"

2. *Ask honest questions.* Sometimes a question can be "loaded" with a message of what the desirable response is (from the point of view of the questioner). Usually, they include a "hidden" opinion disguised as a question. To be intellectually honest, the questioner should state his or her own opinion and then allow the respondent the freedom to agree or disagree. For example, to ask "Don't you think that the main point of the story is compassion?" hides the unstated opinion of the speaker. A more honest or "owned" approach would be something like, "I think that the main point of the story is compassion. What do you think?" or simply "What do you see as the main point of the story?" Questions that are "leading" also thinly veil the intentions of the questioner and put pressure on the respondent to conform. An example of a leading question might be, "Did Jesus want us to love those different from ourselves?" The question is not only closed-ended (asking for a yes or no response) but also one that has an obvious "right" and "wrong" answer. Such questions will tend to stifle discussion by limiting the freedom of the participants. Honest questions are those that are relatively free from imposing a predetermined response on the person responding.

3. *Ask brief questions.* When a question gets very complex with sub-parts and various clauses, participants tend to get confused. If a question becomes too complex, the best strategy may be to break it up into several questions and ask them one at a time. With some careful thought, a complex question may have a central core that forms the one essential or most important question to be asked. Planning ahead and thinking through what might be the main issues or

goals of the discussion will help in selecting and formulating the key questions for the group to consider. For example, the question, "What do you think might have gone through the minds of the priest, the Levite, the Samaritan, and the wounded man when each encountered the latter?" contains several questions. A simpler approach might be to state each question separately, "What do you think might have gone through the mind of the priest when he first encountered the wounded man? . . . What do you think might have gone through the mind of the Samaritan when he first encountered the wounded man?"

4. *Keep your questions focused.* Asking open-ended questions does not imply asking vague or overly broad questions. A question such as "What does this parable tell us?" or "What is Luke's Gospel all about?" may not be very helpful because they are too broad and will probably lead only to superficial answers. A more specific question might be, "What does this passage suggest to you about Jesus' view of the Covenant?" Questions should be specific enough to focus the discussion and open enough to invite a variety of responses.

SUMMARY

The ultimate goal of Scripture study is to help participants deepen their faith in all of its aspects—beliefs, emotional wholeness, and actions. To accomplish this, Scripture study groups need to enable and encourage participants to connect their understandings of the scriptural text with their own life circumstances and lived responses. Participants do this by both listening to the text "in its own voice" with the help of biblical commentaries and listening to God's action in their own life experiences. By integrating the meanings that emerge from both sources, they shape responses for their lives and future actions.

The facilitator's role of posing questions for the group is a key element in the process of integrating scriptural lessons into life responses. Questions that focus on meaning and on response should receive more attention in group discussions than those that simply ask for "facts" in the story. Concretizing questions and questions of balance or congruence are also important in developing the bridge between the meaning of the text and the participants' faith responses.

To be most effective, the facilitator's questions should generally be open-ended, honest, brief, and focused.

REMINDER: Go on to the next page and complete the Question Development Exercise.

NOTES

1. Dick Westley, *Redemptive Intimacy* (Mystic, Conn.: Twenty-Third Publications, 1981).

2. Ibid., 8.

3. The *sensus fidelium* throughout the ages has been recognized by the Church as a valid source of revelation about our Christian faith. Many contemporary theologians are reaffirming it as a primary source for shaping theology.

4. Ibid., 8.

5. Bernhard W. Anderson, *Understanding the Old Testament,* 4th ed. (Englewood Cliffs: Prentice-Hall, 1986) 517–531.

6. For a fuller exploration of the stunning nature of Jesus's parables, see John Dominic Crossan, *The Dark Interval: Towards a Theology of Story* (Allen, Tex.: Argus Communications, 1975).

7. Robert J. Karris, *Invitation to Luke* (Garden City, N.Y.: Image Books, 1977) 135–138.

8. Ibid., 137.

9. Elizabeth Flynn and John LaFaso, *Group Discussion as Learning Process: A Sourcebook* (New York: Paulist Press, 1972) 131.

10. Ibid., 136.

11. Partly adapted from Flynn and LaFaso, 151–155.

QUESTION DEVELOPMENT EXERCISE

Below you will find example questions of Fact, Concretizing, Meaning, Balance, and Response related to the parable of the Good Samaritan (Luke 10:25-37). Add two other questions of your own composition to each of the five categories of questions.

Fact

1. What roles in Jewish society did the two have who passed by the man beaten by the robbers?
2. What actions did the Samaritan take when he saw the beaten man?
3. _____
   _____
4. _____
   _____

Concretizing

1. Who in your experience has proven to be a neighbor or "Good Samaritan" to you?
2. Considering the social structure and boundaries of your own faith community, who might be considered the "Samaritans" or outcasts?
3. _____
   _____
4. _____
   _____

Meaning

1. Do you agree with Robert Karris that this parable is largely about Church membership or who belongs to the People of God? Why or why not?

2. How did your understanding of the parable of the Good Samaritan change or deepen from your first reading of it (see your Pre-Workshop responses) to now?

3. _____

_____

4. _____

_____

Balance or Congruence

1. Which of your ideas or assumptions about God and the People of God does this parable challenge?

2. Does this parable change or challenge the way you view people of other faith? How?

3. _____

_____

4. _____

_____

Response

1. What actions do you feel called to take as a result of studying this passage?

2. What responses and/or changes might this parable call forth from your faith community?

3. _____

_____

4. _____

_____

6
INTEGRATING OUR DIVERSITY

WARM-UP EXERCISES

Before reading the session essay, review the questions and assignments presented below and write your responses in the spaces provided.

A. Reflect and Write:

Recall a recent group experience in which differences among participants became apparent to you.

1. When were you most appreciative of differences among participants in the group?

2. When did you feel uncomfortable or apprehensive about differences among participants in the group?

B. Personality Preference Profile

Differences in personal styles and preferences can often affect how participants interact in a dialogue. The brief assessment below will help you reflect on your interaction style as you read the session essay. An explanation of the four dimensions can be found on pages 78–81.

There are no right or wrong answers to this "test." Simply place an "X" along the lines provided in a way to best characterize your preferences. If your preference is strongly described by one phrase over the other, your X should be close to that descriptive phrase. If you have no strong preference of one phrase over the other, place your X in the middle of the scale.

EXAMPLE

| I hate | 3 | 2 | 1 | 0 | 1 | 2 | 3 | I love |
| ice cream | — | — | — | — | — | — | _X_ | ice cream |

1. I prefer to think out loud as I speak; at parties I like to talk with a lot of people.

   I prefer to think things through before I speak; at parties, I tend to relate to a few rather than a large number of people.

   3 2 1 0 1 2 (3)

   ___ ___ ___ ___ ___ ___ ___

2. I am a good observer of detail. I am down to earth, practical, and rely on the facts of a situation to understand it.

   I trust my hunches. I can see the possibilities in a situation and like to dream about what could happen in the future.

   3 (2) 1 0 1 2 3

   ___ ___ ___ ___ ___ ___ ___

3. I am analytical and logical. When I need to make a decision, I approach it logically. I make decisions with my head.

I often make decisions on the basis of what I feel is the best solution. I make decisions with my heart.

3   2   1   0   1 (2) 3

___ ___ ___ ___ ___ ___ ___

4. I am decisive and rarely waver on decisions. I am generally on-time for meetings.

I tend to be indecisive and take my time in making decisions. I often lose track of time.

3   2   1   0   1 (2) 3

___ ___ ___ ___ ___ ___ ___

Scoring:

Write your "left" of zero scores here:

1. (E) ___
2. (S) _2_
3. (T) ___
4. (J) ___

Write your "right" of zero scores here:

(I) _3_
(N) ___
(F) _2_
(P) _2_

The scores roughly correspond to the four personality preference dimensions that will be described in this session's essay:

Extrovert (E)—Introvert (I)

Sensate (S)—Intuitive (N)

Thinking (T)—Feeling (F)

Judging (J)—Perceiving (P)

The set of questions presented here gives only a "ballpark" profile for the sake of helping you reflect on your own style in group discussions. It is not a tested psychological instrument. For a more in-depth assessment, contact a professional skilled and certified to administer the Myers-Briggs Type Indicator.

C. Reading assignment

1. Read the essay "Integrating Our Diversity" found on the following pages. In the margins note any questions, ideas, or feelings you have in response to the text.

2. Read 1 Corinthians 12:12-26 and reflect on your own experiences of diversity in Christian community.

D. Group Situations Exercise

After reading the session essay, complete the Group Situations Exercise found on pages 90–91.

SESSION ESSAY 6
INTEGRATING OUR DIVERSITY

When we speak of diversity, we highlight our uniqueness and differences from one another. Each of us comes to a group experience with a distinctive personality, family background, cultural heritage, and perspective on life. While we may share many common values and broad traditions (local, national, and religious), we each have a particular point of view and way of interpreting the world in which we find ourselves. These differences make our conversations interesting and enlightening. Diversity breaks monotony and enriches our horizons. Yet, our differences in opinions and styles can also result in conflicts that require special attention and facilitation.

One of the primary tasks of an ongoing group is to integrate the differences in members' styles and perceptions so that dialogue can continue and deepen. Talkative members need to make room for quieter members, and opinionated members need to listen to questioning ones. The facilitator has the task of staying alert to any major imbalances that may occur in the group and of helping the group adjust its patterns, if necessary. When all of the members can appreciate and make room for each others' differences, a healthy and expansive group climate begins to develop. At times, differences may lead to conflict between members, but this, too, if handled well can strengthen the group.

A common assumption that many groups make is to consider all conflict as "bad," to be avoided if possible. But conflict can be quite growthful and creative in groups, especially if it leads to deeper consideration of the issues at hand and if it challenges members to look at their own behaviors. It becomes dysfunctional for a group when participants stop using their basic communication skills and begin violating norms of mutual respect. By the same token when groups try to manage their diverse styles and opinions by becoming overly "nice" with one another, they often lose some of their honesty and authenticity, and the conflict-avoidance itself becomes dysfunctional to the ongoing dialogue. Managing diversity calls for a respectful, honest, and listening stance among all members in the group.

SOURCES OF DIVERSITY

Personal Preferences

Personality theorists have developed scores of tests and descriptions to account for individual differences in relational styles, thought processes, emotional depth, tolerance for ambiguity, and a host of other possible dimensions on which people can differ. I will mention here only a few key dimensions that are particularly relevant to interactions in groups. They relate to the personality dimensions developed by Carl Jung and measured by the Myers-Briggs Type Indicator,[1] an instrument that is often used by ministerial staffs.

Introversion/Extroversion. This dimension relates to the "world" to which the individual is most attuned. *Introverts* are most aware of their own ideas and feelings, spending a good bit of time in the activity of "introspection" or exploring their inner world. *Extroverts,* on the other hand, are attuned to the world around them, their outer world. They often think out loud while speaking to others, whereas introverts tend to prefer to think things through before speaking.

In groups extroverts will often be the first ones to speak. They are more outgoing and have little need to ponder an issue before engaging it in conversation. Introverts may see many implications to a particular statement and will pursue it with inner thought before speaking their mind. Consequently, they often need time to collect their thoughts before jumping into the conversation. A common complaint of introverts is that by the time they want to say something about an issue, the topic of conversation has already moved.

Participants can balance the differences between introverts and extroverts in the group by being sensitive to their needs. Extroverts, for example, may speak readily about the topic at hand but may need some well-designed probing questions to help them reflect more deeply on the topic "out loud." The introverts will benefit by having the discussion questions ahead of time so that they can reflect upon them. Group members, and especially the facilitator, may also need to check to see if those who have not spoken are trying to get into the conversation with little success.

Sensate/Intuitive. Jung's second dimension of personality relates to how a person takes in or perceives information about the world. *Sensate* types tend to rely on their observations and physical senses such as touch, taste, sight, hearing, and smell and can be very detailed in their descriptions of a place, object, or event. They appreciate specific, factual information and can often give precise eye-witness accounts of what they have seen and heard. *Intuitives,* on the other hand, look at situations in terms of their possibilities. They are less concerned with actual events than with the meaning and potential that those events hold. Descriptions of a situation for intuitives are more impressionistic and might focus more, for example, on the mood of a gathering than who was there and what they said.

In discussions, sensate and intuitive participants can often talk past each other. Questions of "fact" and of concretizing (see Chapter 5) may be more appealing to the sensate participants, while questions of meaning and future response and applications are more likely to capture the intuitive's interest. In some groups, conflicts may arise over how much attention to devote to the various types of questions and discussion.[2]

Facilitators and participants might do well to remember that group members differ in their abilities and preferences to remember details, describe events, develop broader insights, and envision future responses. By remaining open to the questions that members may bring to the group, each person has a greater opportunity to gain from the dialogue. Facilitators, in particular, should work toward ensuring that a variety of questions are addressed in the group so that members can each engage at least some of their interests and strengths during the course of the discussion.

Thinking/Feeling. The third dimension in this personal preference theory refers to how people make decisions regarding their perceptions of the world. The thinkers make their judgments about the world through analysis and logic. They often work deductively from general principles and then apply them to particular situations. Fair applications of standards to all is a major concern for those judging through the *thinking* function. People who make their decisions on the basis of *feeling* tend to base them on their most heartfelt values and judge individual situations on the basis of what circumstances surround the event. As can be expected, those higher in feeling tend to express their emotions more readily both verbally and nonverbally.

Without a basis of mutual understanding, the feeling and thinking judgers can begin to judge each other, with thinkers viewing feelers as lacking discipline and logic and the feelers labeling the thinkers as cold and distant. When the group is engaged in discussions which call for decisions of meaning or of response, these differences in how judgments are made are likely to arise. Group members need to remember that they are not required to reach an agreement in a discussion and can allow others to reach conclusions that are different than their own.

Judging/Perceiving. This fourth dimension refers back to the second and third dimensions and asks the question: Does the individual prefer to take in information about the world (*perceiving*) or does the person prefer to make decisions about that information (*judging*)? Those leaning toward the judging end of the scale can make decisions relatively quickly and prefer the sense of "closure" that results from completing a project or coming to a conclusion in a discussion. The ones higher on the perceiving end of the scale enjoy their perceptions and feel little urgency to make a decision. They can always find a new angle of looking at an issue or a new insight. Discussions for the perceiver are rarely ended neatly with a firm and settled decision.

Since perceiving and judging types differ in the orientation to time and closure, their differences will be most apparent in issues involving time and decisions in the group. Punctuality in starting and ending on time, timing of breaks, and time devoted to covering various questions often will be approached more casually by those high on the perceiving scale than by those high on the judging side. The judging participants may also have a greater need to settle a question before moving on to the next.

Since time in the sharing group is limited, the facilitator needs to remind the group of its agreed upon time and discussion norms while being sensitive to making adjustments as group members indicate the desire to do so. Variations from norms (such as deciding to extend the meeting time by fifteen minutes) should be openly acknowledged and negotiated with all members.

Faith Perspectives

The twentieth century has had unparalleled change and growth in technology and global interdependence. We have witnessed the development of telecommunications, jet and space travel, and the computer revolution. One consequence of this massive shift in the structure of our world has been a quantum leap in the number of ways that our experiences can be influenced and touched by others. Whereas members of a congregation may once have been unified not only in their fundamental beliefs but also in their common work experiences, shared world-view, and religious practices, today that is rarely the case. People encounter streams of differing values and opinions through television, books, movies, and travel experiences. Consequently, most congregations are sheaves of variety.

Greg Dues in *Dealing With Diversity*[3] points out that most Catholic parishes today are experiencing some stress arising from the assortment of religious identities that have emerged in the past twenty-five years. Sub-groups in the Church have developed around specific issues, concerns, experiences, or devotions, many of which counter one another. Progressives vie with conservatives, peace and justice and pro-life groups engage in lobbying efforts without much mutual support, and liturgical planners agonize over what kind of music and devotional practices to encourage. The Church is struggling to integrate its diversity.

This is both an exciting and a frightening time for the Church. Old ways are giving way to new, and the hazards and opportunities of change are both evident. In sharing groups, participants' fears, concerns, and frustrations as well as their hopes and dreams will most likely be voiced. Here, as in the larger parish and Church as a whole, managing diversity will be a challenge.

As in any dialogue, *listening* with the aim of mutual understanding is the key for faith-sharing among persons of differing perspectives. Modeling active listening and encouraging others to listen actively to one another is essential, especially in times of heated debate. Beyond that basic principle, members should be encouraged to share not only the conclusions they have reached but also the experiences and processes that have led to those conclusions. If walking in someone's shoes for a while leads to better understanding, we need to know where that walk has been.

At times when differences are accentuated, group members may lose sight of the points of agreement that they share in common. Members who disagree with one another are still part of the wider Church, the Body of Christ. Acknowledging that reality often softens the edges of what might appear to be a sharp disagreement. Indeed, Paul may have been trying to use this approach with differing factions when he used the image of the Body of Christ in 1 Corinthians 12:12-26.

Facilitators can assist members in finding common ground by reflecting back those areas upon which the parties involved can agree. A statement such as, "It seems to me that you both care deeply about preserving Christian tradition in this area but disagree about how to go about it" can clarify the limits of the disagreement and point out the deeper Story and Vision that create a common bond among the participants. The facilitative aim is not to flatten or eliminate disagreements because these often provide the creative energy for deeper reflection. The goal, rather, is to help the participants truly communicate in a spirit of respect, tolerance, and Christian communion.

Cultural Heritage

In our pluralistic society any group that forms is likely to draw members from a variety of cultural and family backgrounds. Differences in this area may fall along a wide but limited range, since we are also shaped in common by our wider contemporary American culture. Even those in our group who come from other countries will communicate with us in an American setting, surrounded by symbols of our local culture. Were we to engage in conversation with them on their own native soil, we would no doubt experience a different sense of dialogue.

Culture provides us with the symbols, language, and assumptions we need to get along readily on a day-to-day basis. It gives us some general rules or guidelines to know what to do, for example, to get into a movie theater or to go to a baseball game. In a different cultural setting, we might find ourselves totally lost in our ability to negotiate the local transport system if a public system even existed.

The assumptions our culture provides also give us guidelines regarding what is proper in relating to others and, at times, whom we should seek out and whom to avoid. Many of these common cultural assumptions need to be challenged when held alongside scriptural mandates. As with most of our foundational assumptions, they are often resistant to change. Thus, the rooting-out process may require considerable effort.

Because we do have some differences in cultural heritage, the assumptions that may be central to one person's world-view may be only peripheral or unimportant to another. Both patience and openness are called for among all members—patience when someone becomes defensive of a particular stance and openness when having our own unquestioned assumptions put to the test. These two attitudes are particularly important as we work toward developing community, while we dialogue about the meaning that scriptural texts hold for our lives.

SOME GUIDELINES FOR TIMES OF CONFLICT

Third-Party Interventions

Heated conflict situations may be rare in many Christian study groups, but when they occur, they have some predictable consequences. As emotional temperatures rise, the people participating in the disagreement tend to lose some of their ability to listen with empathy. Distortions of words and meaning become common, and the parties involved often begin to hear the other person's message selectively—coloring words in their worst possible connotations and ignoring parts of the message that seem more positive and indicative of areas of agreement.

In many cases the participants can work through the disagreement themselves without the help of the facilitator if they are skilled in listening. However, sometimes two or more participants may get "stuck" in a deadlock of differing viewpoints, taking up much of the group's time. The facilitator can intervene in such disagreements to help the parties clarify, listen to one another, and resolve, if possible, the source of their conflict. Such facilitative actions are commonly called *third-party interventions* because the facilitator is entering into the scene as a "third" person or point of view to the conflict. Some guidelines for this kind of intervention are provided below. The disagreements requiring all four steps of the process will probably be rare. Most discussions can be set back on track with the use of Steps 1 and 2. However, all four steps are presented here for the sake of completion.

Step 1: State Your Observations. In the midst of an argument, the facilitator first needs to get into the conversation to be able to speak. This may be no small task and may call for breaking in tactfully in the middle of the discussion. The facilitator's first comments are usually a reflection of what the facilitator observes and senses is happening among the conflicting parties. It is important that the facilitator model effective communication skills, especially the use of I-language, as he or she intervenes. An example of an opening statement is presented below. Notice that it reflects underlying feelings as well as observations.

> It seems to me that you are both feeling quite upset about your differences on this issue. I hear you both stating your position with passionate conviction, but I'm not sure that you are really listening to each other because I hear no one stopping to paraphrase or acknowledge common ground. I'd like to suggest that we back up for a moment and clarify where you agree and disagree with each other. Are you willing to do that?

The statement ends with a question asking if the parties are open to an intervention. They may simply respond by restating their position, but the facilitator should be assertive in asking for a response to the question posed. Most persons when pressed will not choose a response of "No, we would rather engage in a endless argument."

Step 2: Invite each person to state his or her position and underlying interests or values. A person's position in a conflict is often like the punchline of a joke. It is the conclusion of a long set of considerations. For example, I may want to hold our meetings at someone's home because the parking lot is not well lit at the parish hall, and I'm reluctant to park there alone at night. Another person might hold the position that meetings should be held at the parish hall because of its central location. If we only say what our positions are—meet in a home versus meet at the parish hall—our differences may seem to be irreconcilable. But if we each know one another's underlying interests, we can work toward a mutually agreeable solution—finding a home or other meeting place that is centrally located and has a well lit parking area.

The facilitator should begin by stating some of the ground rules or procedures that he or she is proposing and then proceed to invite each person to speak without interruption. When giving each of the conflicting parties a chance to speak, the facilitator should encourage them to state the full story—both their position and any underlying interests, values, beliefs, or experiences that are making that position compelling for them. Facilitators should also ask them to be brief in this initial statement. If anyone interrupts the speaker during this time, the facilitator should assertively ask the interrupter to hold comments until each person has had a chance to speak.

Step 3: Invite each person to restate what the other person has said. Research in communication has repeatedly found a tendency among conflicting parties to distort or omit important pieces of information during times of heated disagreement. The facilitator can help the persons involved overcome this deficit by asking them to engage in reflective listening with empathy for the other person's unique experiences and situation. An example facilitative statement at this point might be, "Now that you have each had an opportunity to clarify your position, I ask that you acknowledge your understanding of one another's statements by paraphrasing what you heard."

Step 4: Help the parties acknowledge their common ground and identify the crux of the disagreement. The facilitator here can use a variety of probing and reflective statements to help the conflicting parties name their areas of agreement and identify the main source of their conflict. The facilitator should check on some common sources that might be cleared up readily:

- Are the people involved talking about the same thing? Or are they using similar words in very different contexts (a problem of semantics)?

- Would some additional information help? (For example, a disagreement over whether the parable of the prodigal son is found in Luke's or in John's gospel could be easily solved by checking.)

Summary statements that reflect the main points of the conversation are usually quite helpful during this clarification stage. If the conflict is one that calls for a group decision, arriving at a clear statement of the problem is crucial. For example, after identifying and clarifying the various parties' interests, the facilitator might pose the following statement, "It seems to me that the problem is one of finding a meeting place that is centrally located and that offers ample lighting in the parking area." Once the problem is stated in terms of all the underlying interests, problem solving can generally proceed smoothly.

Not all conflicts lend themselves to win-win solutions, however. Sometimes the disagreement is rooted in values or beliefs that neither party will compromise. If the disagreement occurs as part of a dialogue, there is no need to work on a common solution. The parties may "agree to disagree" but should do so having at least heard each other's stories and reasoning. The facilitator might move the discussion on by summarizing the main points each person has made and acknowledging that some real differences remain. If the differences are part of a decision-making discussion, the group may need to find a solution that at least will not violate each person's primary values. The final solution may not be anyone's first choice, but it should be a solution that everyone can "live with."

Calling Members to Accountability

Sometimes tension may arise in the group, not because two or more people are in disagreement, but because one or more participants are violating an explicit or even implicit norm. One member may consistently come to the group unprepared or another may frequently interrupt others to make a point. Whatever the norm violation, it should be addressed if it is affecting the communal bonds or effectiveness of the group.

In groups that have developed trust and honesty over a long period of time, participants may readily call other members to the accountability they have pledged one another. In earlier stages of group development, however, group members are often afraid of "rocking the boat" and will leave the task of addressing group norm issues to the facilitator.

Facilitators should remember that their first line of bringing members back to agreed upon norms need not be a direct statement to the individual involved. Time spent at the end of a session inviting participants to assess how the session went and to review some of the norms will go a long way in preventing problems from occurring. The facilitator, for example, might ask participants to share with one or two other persons what they consider to be their own strengths and weaknesses in contributing to the dialogue. This semi-public "examination of conscience" helps members to recall their own facilitative behaviors and affirm them. Inviting members both to ask for and to give each other feedback on group participation also helps to reinforce honesty and a sharing of responsibility for the well-being of the group. If addressing a particular members' behavior is still warranted, the following guidelines might prove helpful:

1. Affirm the person's strengths. Many seemingly disruptive behaviors stem from an overabundance of a particular strength. The person in the group, for example, who dominates by talking too much may have many insights and a strong interest in the topic at hand. The quiet member may be a good listener and be overly reluctant to jump into the conversation for fear of interrupting another person. Balancing or toning down a strength is usually an easier challenge to manage than compensating for a deficit.

2. State the problem behavior and its effect on you. The one who gives feedback should describe specifically what the person is doing and how that behavior is experienced. By doing so, the speaker gives a clear picture of what the issue is and why it is problematic. As with all personal statements, the individual should use I-language in stating perceptions and effects.

3. State specifically what changes you would like to see. Simply pointing out a problem behavior does not give a person a clear indication of what the speaker wants instead. A clear description of the desired changes in behavior will make the change process easier and leaves room for some negotiation to meet both parties' needs. Some examples are:

> John, I have noticed that you have a lot of experiences that relate to this particular passage of Scripture. I hear your enthusiasm in the many things you are telling us. I am also concerned that our time is limited and many others in the group have not had a chance to speak. Would you be willing to summarize briefly the main insights you have gained from your experiences?

*   *   *

> Martha, when others are speaking I notice how your facial expressions show that you are connecting well with what they are saying. Sometimes, I hear you jump in with a similar story of your own before they have had a chance to finish, and I feel anxious because I want to hear both of you. Would you be willing to wait until each person has finished before telling us your experiences?

*   *   *

> Bill, I appreciated your honesty in challenging Sue. I also found myself feeling somewhat defensive because I heard your comments as labels rather than as observations. I would find your feedback more helpful if you could use I-statements and be more specific in saying what Sue is doing rather than speaking of her attitudes. It might be good to check with Sue about how she is hearing your message.

SUMMARY

Our diversity is the source of creative and lively dialogue and at times of conflict. Conflict, in and of itself, is not destructive of community and can certainly lead to deeper levels of reflection. Only when conflicting parties fail to listen and communicate respectfully with one another does conflict become a source of erosion to community.

Our differences from one another stem from various influences on our lives. In this essay we have explored some of the variations in personal preference, faith perspectives, and cultural heritage that can affect group dynamics. These differences call for tolerance, patience, and openness among all group members as well as for skillfulness in third-party interventions by the facilitator.

When a facilitator assists two or more people in a conflict to clarify and resolve their differences, he or she might use the steps involved in third-party intervention. When challenging a member to follow norms that were agreed upon by group members, the facilitator might find it useful to follow the guidelines for calling members to accountability. The facilitator can also help to prevent problems from occurring in the group by periodically inviting group members to reflect on their progress in living out their group norms.

REMINDER: Read 1 Corinthians 12:12-26 and reflect on your own experiences of diversity in Christian community. Also, complete the Group Situations Exercise found on pages 90–91.

NOTES

1. Myers-Briggs Type Indicator (Palo Alto: Consulting Psychologists Press). For further information on the four personality dimensions measured by this instrument, see Isabel Brigge Myers with Peter B. Myers, *Gifts Differing* (Palo Alto: Consulting Psychologists Press, 1980).

2. The sensate/intuitive division is not the only personal preference dimension that can result in a difference in interest level for various discussions. Some members may prefer a more academic and theoretical tone to the discussion while others may prefer an experience-based, practical focus. The difference in abstract versus concrete learning styles is another dimension of personal difference that has been researched, for example, by Kolb. See David A. Kolb, *The Learning Style Inventory* (Boston: McBer and Company, 1976).

3. Greg Dues, *Dealing with Diversity: A Guide for Parish Leaders* (Mystic: Conn.: Twenty-Third Publications, 1988).

GROUP SITUATIONS EXERCISE

For each of the situations presented below, write as accurately as possible your actual statements or the actions you would take in response to the participant's words or behavior. If you would say or do nothing leave the space blank.

1. Tom, a member of your group, repeatedly makes remarks that imply that his way is the only correct way of viewing things. He has just said to the group, "Anyone who can't see that this parable applies to parish council meetings probably just didn't read it very well." What would you say or do?

_____

_____

_____

2. Alice goes on and on with great detail in expressing personal stories that relate to the biblical passage under consideration. She has just spoken for about four minutes and seems to be nowhere near the point of her story. What would you say or do?

_____

_____

_____

3. Peter has just mentioned at the beginning of the session that he didn't do any of the readings or assigned questions during the week. He said something similar at the beginning of last week's session and has not seemed to be prepared for several other weeks. What would you say or do?

_____

_____

_____

4. Sarah is usually quiet but has just challenged another member of the group for the first time. Her comment was, "I agree with

your conclusion but I arrived at that point from a very different path. . . ." What would you say or do?

_____

_____

_____

5. Gerry has just interrupted a speaker for the third time. Each time the speakers allowed her to speak without finishing their statements. What would you say or do?

_____

_____

_____

7
TUNING INTO GROUP LIFE

WARM-UP EXERCISES

Before reading the session essay, review the questions and assignments presented below and write your responses in the spaces provided.

A. Reflect and Write:

Think of a small group in which you participated over an ex-
tended period of time.

1. How would you describe the "personality" of the group as a
   whole? (e.g., if this group were a person, what kind of personality would it have?)

2. If you were to compare this group to an animal, which one
   would you choose? (e.g., lion? puppy? fox? owl? centipede?)
   What characteristics of the group led you to make this choice
   of imagery?

B. Reading and reflection assignment:

1. Read Ephesians 4:1-6. What meaning might this passage have for an on-going faith-sharing group?

2. Read the essay "Tuning Into Group Life" found on the following pages. In the margins note any questions, ideas, or feelings you have in response to the text.

SESSION ESSAY 7

TUNING INTO GROUP LIFE

"The whole is greater than the sum of its parts" is much more than a math principle. It points to the necessity of looking at things in terms of the whole, "wholistically," if we want to understand them as fully as possible.

I can examine a rose in terms of its color, in terms of its biological structure, or even by means of its molecular composition. But as poet Gertrude Stein says, "A rose is a rose is a rose." Unless I can appreciate the rose without analyzing its individual parts, I will never really know the rose.

Groups have a life, a personality, of their own. They may be made up of individuals, but unless I can tune into the life of the group as a whole, I will not know it as "group." Instead, I will see it only as a collection of individual participants. To understand the group, I must move beyond the level of individual behaviors and look for broader patterns of interaction that characterize the mood and life of the group as a whole.

Until now the essays in this book have been focusing largely on the specific skills of individuals in the group. Now, I would like to share with you some ways of looking at the *patterns* of behaviors that form the warp and woof of the group's life. Several approaches are available for examining these patterns, and some may be more useful than others at various points in the group's development.

NORMS

We have already explored the importance of maintaining healthy group norms, the "ground rules" that guide members' actions in the small-group meeting. Besides providing standards for accountability and honesty, norms enacted in the group can disclose the tone and emotional climate of the group's life.

While most groups have a set of explicitly stated guidelines that shape the structure of their meetings, they generally have an untold number of *implicit* norms that are not stated verbally. These unspoken norms nevertheless define what the group considers to be appropriate or "acceptable" behavior. Groups tend to exert a considerable amount of pressure, both subtle and overt, on their members to conform to these established norms. Often, group members will become visibly agitated when a valued norm is violated.

If Mary, for example, began pacing the floor while others sat in a circle during a discussion, she would probably be engaging in actions outside of the range of acceptable member behavior. The behavior itself would likely be distracting to the other group members because of its strangeness in this setting. Moreover, breaking the unspoken norm of remaining seated during the discussion would evoke anxiety among some of the members expressed through their eye contact and posture. To reduce this anxiety, someone may eventually say something to Mary or the group may simply ignore her presence, in essence redefining the group to those who keep the norms. On the other hand, group members may grow to accept this behavior as normal for Mary. In this case, a new norm of what is considered acceptable may be established.

We generally feel no need to list out all the behaviors that will be deemed appropriate or inappropriate in a group. Our cultural norms already provide much of the guidance for members as to what is considered "normal" group behavior. Within those broad guidelines, each group will also develop its own set of acceptable patterns that will make it distinct, even among other groups that are discussing the same content material.

Degree of Formality

Groups, for example, differ in the degree of formality that members exhibit with one another. Determined by a variety of factors such as cultural setting, length of acquaintance, educational background, and socioeconomic status, the degree of formality or informality in the group creates a characteristic tone to the flow of conversation in the dialogue. Most faith-sharing groups, of course, tend to be fairly informal, placing a high value on friendship and warmth. Nevertheless, if we were to visit a number of these groups in different settings, we would probably notice some variations along this dimension.

The physical setting for the group meeting often gives cues as to the degree of formality expected among group members. If the meeting takes place in a formal living room where members wear suits and "Sunday" clothes, the interactions may be different than if members meet in a casual den or in a parish hall. Facilitators should note the effects of settings on the group's life and choose meeting places that allow participants to be both comfortable and attentive to their purpose for gathering.

Use of Time

The use of time by a group is generally easy to observe, because we have a standard, the clock, to use as a measuring device. Some groups are highly punctual—beginning and ending on time, using only the allotted time for breaks, and managing their distribution of time for various discussion questions. If Tom were to walk into the meeting three minutes late in such a group, his tardiness would likely be felt as a norm violation.

In other groups the members arrive over a period of time, socializing for a while and beginning when everyone is ready. Their ending time is flexible, and mingling during breaks may be as important as discussing the assignments. Both groups may have healthy norms in terms of accomplishing the purposes of the program and meeting group members' needs. The difference lies with the group's composition and the interests of the members.

Norms surrounding the use of time become problematic for groups when some members want to start and end at a leisurely pace and others expect to begin and end on time. Timing norms may also become counter-productive if the members want to take long breaks but still end the meeting at the appointed time. With these norms in place, the participants' progress in their study program would likely suffer. When group members use time in a way that does not serve their explicit purpose, they need to clarify their norms in light of their goals, interests, and circumstances.

Interaction Patterns

If we were to watch a number of groups interact, we might observe several distinctive patterns of communication. By watching how persons in the group direct their eye contact and exchange questions and responses, we might notice, for example, that in one group each of the members seems to focus eye contact on one or two key members. In another, each person participates in the discussion and looks at all of the others while speaking. The first group's pattern is typical of a beginning group, where members are looking largely to the facilitator for guidance and direction. The second fits a pattern of a well-developed group that has included each of its members as equal partners.

Other patterns can also emerge. Three or four members may interact enthusiastically with each other while other members occasionally say something to those in this "inner" circle. Such a pattern may indicate that some members have become full-fledged participants while others have taken the role of observers to the discussion. If this pattern continues as the "norm," the group may never become fully integrated or experience the benefit of shared insights from all members.

Watching the interaction patterns of a group can give the facilitator a quick indication of the group's stage of development. If the group appears to be stuck, the facilitator can help the group make some needed adjustments by naming the problem for the group and suggesting some possible corrective actions. By selectively teaching group members how to observe their patterns of interaction, the facilitator can empower participants to correct these imbalances on their own.

STAGES OF DEVELOPMENT

Like individuals, groups grow in maturity and depth, and they move through fairly predictable stages of development. In the fifties psychologist Will Schutz[1] proposed that groups move through three phases of growth which he named *inclusion, control,* and *affection.* In each stage, the group faces a developmental issue that is often addressed non-verbally and unconsciously as members engage in their weekly discussions. Members need to resolve the development task of each stage before they can progress to the next.

Inclusion

During the *inclusion* phase, the group's task is to include everyone in the life of the group. Many of the group norms are not yet established, and members are cautious about doing anything that might cause their exclusion from the group. Some members may prefer not to be fully included, remaining in the observer position until they feel "safe" enough to join. Others may have a high need for inclusion and feel anxious if they are left out of the conversation. Because of the lack of firmly established norms in this stage, the group tends to be highly dependent on the facilitator for guidance and direction.

The facilitator can help the group resolve inclusion issues by clarifying expectations and by affirming that each member shares in the responsibility for maintaining a healthy group. The facilitator should also consistently model inclusive behavior by directing eye contact to all members in the group and by encouraging others to do the same. Session 2, Getting Started offers a variety of suggestions for assisting groups during this inclusion phase.

Control

Once the composition of the group has been determined, the group's concern moves on to a new issue to be resolved—who will *control* the group. Questions emerge such as who will be the most influential in the group and whose ideas will predominate. Some members may try to dominate the conversation by not letting others speak or by speaking louder than others. Others may yield control by refusing to challenge the more dominant members.

If the norm of shared power is to be established, the facilitator needs to challenge both the dominators and the quiet members to balance their use of influence in the group. Often, the facilitator helps to restore equal sharing simply by reminding the entire group of their purpose and group agreement. At other times the facilitator may need to confront the parties involved. The facilitator, in a sense, is a model and teacher of how to share power. The learning process may require a considerable amount of time since power-sharing runs counter to many of the messages that our larger society reinforces.

Affection

The third stage that Schutz mentions is that of *affection*. When the group has successfully resolved its control issues with honesty and grace, trust and empathy begin to break through. Members hear one another's stories with compassion, and bonds of friendship and closeness form. This is the stage where community becomes a felt reality.

This stage, however, also requires some work. Bonding may occur among sub-groups first, with the potential danger of forming cliques rather than full community. Some members may be less comfortable in this stage where emotional ties require more risk and vulnerability. The facilitator's ability to sense and reflect feelings is especially important at this stage. As members search for ways of becoming more open with one another, the facilitator can help with skillful active listening.

Other Stages

Researchers that followed Schutz have developed a variety of theories of group development stages. Schutz's three phases are generally included as basic, but most social psychologists[2] recognize at least two other stages of group growth.

The fourth is usually called the *performance* phase where the purpose and task of the group becomes central. Having resolved much of its internal emotional work, the group focuses outward with a highly motivated team spirit to get its primary task accomplished. In Scripture study groups this may be a time of increased learning and sharing and may also be a time when members start working more energetically toward applying their insights to real life situations. In some cases, the group as a whole may want to develop a ministry project together.

The fifth stage is that of *ending* the group experience. Much more will be said about this challenge in the next chapter. As learning groups approach the end of their course, they need to make some decisions. Should they continue? Should they disband? Perhaps only some members would like to continue, and the group will reform without some of the key participants who gave it life. The emotional issues evoked by times of leaving bring the group back to an internal focus and move members to resolve their unfinished business.

Different groups will vary greatly in the amount of time they spend in each stage and how they go about resolving developmental issues. Schutz suggests that groups may also move through several stages and then recycle back through earlier stages to reach deeper levels of resolution. A change in group life, such as the addition or loss of a group member, may further shift the developmental task of the group. If the facilitator can remain alert to the group's underlying developmental issues, he or she will be more effective in helping the group grow and mature.

SHARED FACILITATION

The facilitator's aim throughout the group's life is to empower members to become cofacilitators, skilled in maintaining the health of the group. The facilitator accomplishes this goal by modeling facilitative behavior, inviting observations on group issues, and affirming comments made by members that seem helpful to the group. In established groups, a new observer might find it difficult to determine who the designated facilitator is since a number of participants may be skillfully facilitating the discussion.

One way of examining the level of shared responsibility in the group is to notice who and how many participants are engaging in facilitative behaviors. This type of observation can be done informally, but because it involves a large number of activities and people, it is often done in a more disciplined way by recording which participants demonstrate specific facilitative actions. Broadly, these actions are divided into *task-oriented behaviors* (which help the group stay on task) and *group maintenance behaviors* (which help group members communicate well with one another and develop a sense of community).[3]

Task-Oriented Behaviors

Initiating. Discussions develop only when someone is willing to plunge in and respond to the question at hand. Initiators provide the spark that often ignites a lively and thoughtful dialogue. They facilitate the discussion by directly addressing the question and by "breaking the ice" so that others are encouraged to follow. Example: "I had some thoughts on that first question. What this passage means to me is . . . ."

Providing Information. Others that add to the discussion by providing their thoughts, feelings, and opinions are also contributing to the group's purpose and are thereby facilitating the discussion. By keeping to the topic, they are focusing the group on its primary task. Example: "Yes, I can't think of a better way to speak about our relatedness than to say that we are all part of one body. . . ."

Seeking Information. The one who poses discussion and follow-up questions to the group is leading the group into dialogue. When group members use the active listening skill of probing for more information, they are helping others enter more deeply into the conversation. Example: "What do you mean when you say 'relatedness?' "

Clarifying or Elaborating. A member who clarifies what another is saying by either paraphrasing or expanding upon the ideas expressed helps the group achieve fuller understandings of one another's meanings and facilitates listening for the entire group. Example: "It sounds like you are saying that we cannot ignore the sufferings of others because if one suffers, the entire 'body' feels it. . . ."

Summarizing. At key points in a discussion, a summary statement is sometimes useful in helping the group take stock of its progress. Although they are not always necessary at transitions, summaries can allow the group to develop a sense of completion before moving on to a new activity. Example: "In this discussion, we seem to have focused on three possible interpretations for Paul's use of the image 'body.' The first is . . . ."

Testing for Consensus. When the group is making a consensus decision (a decision that everyone can "live with"), the person who checks with participants to see if they all truly agree is testing for consensus. Sometimes, a group seems to be reaching a consensus but in reality is far from agreement. Silence may have been interpreted as consent, whereas many of the silent members may not be expressing their reservations. Careful testing for consensus will usually guard against false group decisions. Example: "If you would like to change the meeting day from Tuesday to Wednesday, please say 'Yes.' I suggest that we go around the circle and hear from everyone. . . ."

Group-Maintenance Behaviors

Gatekeeping. Gatekeeping behavior ensures that everyone who wants to speak gets a chance to say something to the group. The gatekeeper watches for signs of others' unsuccessful attempts to get "air time" in the group and acknowledges the members' efforts. Example: "Sue, you look like you've been wanting to jump into this conversation for awhile now."

Encouraging. When we encourage another in the group, we affirm the value of their contributions and invite them to continue participating. Often the encouraging is done non-verbally with attentive expressions and nodding. An example of a verbal encouraging statement is: "I really appreciate your sharing that story. It means a lot to me. . . ."

Harmonizing. Without discounting real differences, a harmonizing statement can acknowledge what common ground exists and offer possible avenues of solution or compromise. Example: "You both seem to be expressing a concern for faithfulness to early Christian roots. Perhaps you are each expressing a different but important dimension of what faithfulness means?"

Expressing Group Feeling. When group members seem to be sharing a common experience or feeling, the person who acknowledges and names the emotion for the group brings to consciousness what is perhaps below the surface and enables the group to take action if necessary. Example: "I sense that many of us are feeling tired. Perhaps we should take our break now and continue with our discussion in ten minutes?"

Pointing Out Communication Patterns. As group members become skilled in living out their group agreement and in using basic communication skills, they can call others to communicate more effectively. Example: "I think we are getting into a habit of interrupting one another. I'd like to suggest that we each let others finish what they are saying before we speak."

Standard Setting. When a person suggests a procedure for how the group might approach a problem or engage in discussion, he or she is standard setting. Example: "Could we take a few minutes to reflect quietly on this question before we begin discussing it?"

SUMMARY

To understand and to help maintain a healthy group life, the facilitator needs to observe the group as a whole—its patterns of interaction and its unconscious struggles in developing into maturity. Several approaches are available for tuning into group life "wholistically."

One way is to note the kind of norms that are guiding group behaviors. Norms that emphasize participation, openness, and mutual accountability help the group to accomplish its purpose. Other norms may develop that run counter to the group's agreed upon goals and should be pointed out for the group's attention and consideration.

Another way of perceiving group life is to observe the kinds of underlying issues that the group is experiencing. Social psychologists point out at least five different stages of group development centering on the issues of inclusion, control, affection, performance, and closure of the group.

Finally, a group can be examined in terms of its pattern of sharing power and facilitative behaviors. Members who help the group stay on task or who foster communication among members become cofacilitators for the group. When all members share these functions, the participants have become responsible partners in maintaining a healthy group atmosphere.

NOTES

1. William C. Schutz, *The Interpersonal Underworld* (Palo Alto: Science and Be-havior Books, 1966), first copyrighted in 1958 by William Schutz and published as *FIRO: A Three-Dimensional Theory of Interpersonal Behavior* (New York: Holt, Rinehart & Winston, 1960).

2. Tuckman and Jensen reviewed much of the literature on stages of group development and summarized the five primary stages as those of *forming, storming, norming, performing,* and *adjourning.* See B. W. Tuckman & M.A.C. Jensen, "Stages of small group development revisited," *Group and Organizational Studies,* 1977, *2,* 419–427. More recent discussions of stages of group development can be found in D. R. Forsyth, *Group Dynamics,* 2nd ed. (Pacific Grove, Calif.: Brooks/Cole, 1990) and M. S. Corey and G. Corey, *Groups: Process and Practice,* 4th ed., (Pacific Grove, Calif.: Brooks/Cole, 1992).

3. Based on K. D. Benne and P. Sheats, "Functional Roles of Group Members," *Journal of Social Issues* (1948) 2:42–47.

8
GROUP TRANSITIONS

WARM-UP EXERCISES

Before reading the session essay, review the questions and assignments presented below and write your responses in the spaces provided.

A. Reflect and Write:

1. What experiences have you had with times of transition in the life of a group (e.g., loss or addition of a member, end of group, etc.)? What helped or hindered the group in those moments?

2. What have you learned as a result of these sessions that will help you most as a facilitator?

3. How might this learning experience apply to other relationships in your life?

4. What questions do you still have about facilitating groups?

5. How will you continue to gather information and develop the facilitation skills you need?

B. Reading and reflection assignment:

1. Read the essay "Group Transitions" found on the following pages. In the margins, note any questions, ideas, or feelings you have in response to the text.

2. Read James 2:14-26. What challenges do you hear in this passage for faith-sharing communities?

SESSION ESSAY 8
GROUP TRANSITIONS

Perhaps nothing is more constant in our twentieth century living than change. People move, they change jobs, their children grow and leave home, and they develop new priorities as their perspectives grow. All of these external circumstances can affect the energies given to group participation, and the group itself can change.

Change is a major source of stress. It is also the central reality of conversion and growth. Groups who want to grow in Christian faith and commitment need to welcome opportunities for change with a willingness to work through all the feelings, implications, and issues that transitional periods evoke. How the group handles times of transition will determine whether the group becomes transformed and unified or strained and splintered.

Chapter 7 explored a group's movements through stages of development and the issues that members must deal with effectively if they are to grow. This chapter will focus on some of the common changes that groups undergo during their lifetimes and offer suggestions to foster growth during those times of uncertainty and possibility. Specifically, we will consider the issues that emerge when (a) a new member joins the group, (b) a member leaves the group, (c) the group experience comes to an end, and (d) the group's original purpose expands or changes, transforming the group into a new entity.

INCLUDING A NEW MEMBER

As Chapter 7 pointed out, in the initial stage of the group's life, each person "tests the waters" to find the limits of acceptable behaviors and expressions. Gradually, trust develops as participants learn that others will receive what they have to say with respect and confidentiality. Through continual experiences of acceptance and trustworthiness in the group, members feel "safe" enough to open themselves to deeper levels of sharing, and the group bonds into true community.

Any change in membership of the group constitutes a new "personality" for the community. When a new member is added, the anxieties and questions of the inclusion stage surface again for both the new member and the original members of the group. Since group trust is only as strong as its weakest link, the new member often represents an "unknown" element that may disturb some of the group's existing security. The web of trust among members needs to extend its weave to include relationships with the new member.

The facilitator can help the group assimilate the new member into its life more readily by creating opportunities to dispel the unknowns for both the new member and the original group. Questions that arise at this time often include: Who is this person? Who is this group? What is expected here? How will this person relate to me? Will our ease and patterns of communicating with one another change? While participants can rarely answer these questions directly, they should allow time in their meetings to get acquainted with the new member and to explore the implications of expanding the group.

When a person expresses interest in joining an existing group, the facilitator should consult the group. Since ownership of group life belongs to all the members, any decision to change it should be made jointly. If members have no objection to including the person, the facilitator's next step is to provide an initial orientation for the new member. The facilitator should review the purpose of the group, its explicit norms and expectations, and general ways of proceeding, allowing the new member time to ask questions and clarify any previous conceptions held. Sometimes, a person may have experienced a very different format for group meetings called "Scripture study" or "faith-sharing" and may expect this group to function the same way. Giving the person the opportunity to clarify potential misunderstandings before actually coming into the group will save much time and possible embarrassment and enable the new person to make an informed decision about joining.

At the new member's first meeting with the group, all should introduce themselves, perhaps adding some interesting information such as what this group experience has meant for them. (The newcomer could express what he or she hopes to gain by joining the group.) In well established groups that have a long-standing history together, members might also tell the "story" of the group with its high and low points, struggles and insights. The newcomer might also want to ask questions of group members regarding their group experience.

Often, the group meets and welcomes the new member at a shared meal or in an informal social gathering. Whatever the approach chosen, hospitality and openness should be the primary themes. When this "getting acquainted" period is completed and initial questions have been raised and answered, the group can proceed with its task, making sure to include the new member in its discussions.

LOSING A MEMBER

Life circumstances sometimes change unexpectedly, causing an early leave for a member who may have intended to stay with the group throughout its duration. As happens when the group adds a member, the tone and patterns of communications shift when the group loses a member. But the emotional effect on the group can be even more profound as the group and departing member experience feelings of loss and, at times, grief. People need room to work through unfinished business and express the emotions evoked by separations. Even if the person is not leaving the area and may see group members in other settings, the community that has developed around this particular group life will not be the same.

If the member has been a vital and accepted member of the group, the unfinished business will be somewhat different than if the member has been engaged in continual conflict within the group. In either case, there is a need for emotional space and opportunity for healing. Both the member and the group can benefit from acknowledging their feelings and resolving as best they can the issues that press upon them.

The facilitator's main task is to encourage members to be aware of their emotions and to express them honestly. When the facilitator first learns of the member's plans to leave the group, he or she should encourage the member to speak to the entire group if the person has not already done so. Within the session, the facilitator should encourage members to speak directly to the departing person if they wish to say anything about their sense of caring or loss. If conflict has been present, old arguments will not readily be resolved, but members might acknowledge honestly what the conflict itself has meant to them, affirming whatever strengths they are able to at this time. The facilitator might also invite the person leaving to share what the group has meant and what he or she has valued most.

Departures can be a major life change for the group. As with other life changes, time may be the primary healer of the resulting grief and emotion. However, symbolizing the group's experience through ritual and prayer may help both the departing member and the group move on. The facilitator might encourage members to plan their own service, celebrating group members' gifts to one another and their hopes for the future.

ENDING A GROUP

The issues of separation are multiplied many times over when the entire group experience comes to an end. Most members will probably feel some loss and sadness mixed with a host of other feelings related to ending the entire group experience. Again, the facilitator's main task is to enable and encourage members to express their feelings openly and to deal with their unfinished business.

Depending on the length of the group's time together, the resolution of separation issues may require several sessions. The facilitator, for example, might allow some time at the end of a meeting to ask members if they would like to plan a closing ceremony, meal, or service. In this initial discussion, he or she can be responsive to members' expressions of feeling and use active listening skills to explore their depth and meaning. The facilitator can also encourage members to express their emotions by expressing his or her own feelings about the coming separation.

The end-time of a group is also a time for summarizing what has been learned. During the group's last session, the facilitator should set aside ample time for participants to review their group experience. Questions that might be posed to the group include: What insights have you gained through this group experience? What were the turning points for you, both in your own personal growth and in the life of the group? What did you like best and least about being in this group? How would you describe the history of this group? What were the highlights of our group life together? As members reflect on their group experience, the facilitator should encourage specific rather than vague answers to questions. If a person says, for example, "I learned a lot about the early Christian communities," the facilitator might respond with, "Can you tell us what impressed you most about these communities?"

In planning for the future, groups may want to consider possibilities beyond their closing ceremony. If continuing the group is not feasible, members may still want to meet periodically, perhaps once a month, to share their ongoing growth and insights. Members should be honest in their intentions, however, and not create visions of monthly meetings that in reality they will not be able to attend.

TRANSFORMING THE GROUP

Christian groups who form for one specific purpose sometimes expand or shift their scope of activities as they grow and deepen in their faith. Prayer groups may become study groups; study groups may begin engaging in social action together. Regardless of the group's original purpose, the group and facilitator need to discern how the Spirit is moving in the group and respond to the urging for transformation. While many examples can be given, this section focuses primarily on the transformation of Scripture study groups.

Many people first join Scripture study groups because of a thirst for biblical knowledge and a hunger for community. They want to know more about the roots of their Christian commitment and often join with others to pursue prayerfully a deeper understanding of their faith. Others join because of curiosity or because of promptings from friends or spouses. Regardless of their original reasons for joining, group members often experience a new light dawning as they enter into dialogue with Scripture. Through their study of the prophets, the Gospels, and early Christian communities, they may catch a glimpse of Christian community that goes beyond their current experiences, and with that vision, they begin to hunger and thirst for the justice and peace (*shalom*) of God.

Scripture study continually invites us into a dialogue between biblical themes and our own lived experience. Often what we first seek and find in Scripture is an encounter with a living God who loves us unconditionally and calls us into relationship. We also find lessons and examples that can be applied to our own individual lives and circumstances. But as we move deeper into Scripture, we discover a call for *communal* conversion that goes beyond the invitation for individual change. As this occurs, the Scripture study group as a whole may find itself called into conversion and transformation together as a community.

The Call to Holiness

In the Old Testament we find that God relates to Israel as a people and continually calls not only for a personal holiness but also, and most insistently, for a social and communal dimension of holiness. Although rugged individualism pervades our modern mentality, it is absent in the Judeo-Christian tradition. God always calls a *people* to holiness.

Throughout the prophetic writings of the Old Testament, God calls the entire people to create a social reality that preserves the dignity and basic needs of all. When the people fail to create a society based on justice and compassion, they are alienated from God— the reality we call "sin." In Jesus' preaching and ministry, too, we find similar themes. His public life begins with the formation of community (the Twelve and other disciples) and his healings are social as well as physical and spiritual. In the gospel-healing stories, Jesus restores outcasts to a full and dignified place in the community (e.g., Luke 6:13-14) and calls others to do the same (Matt 25:31-46).

The Pastoral Constitution on the Church, written as a document of the Vatican Council II, directs us as Church to continue Jesus' ministry of bringing about the reign of God. It calls us to transform the world's social order that it may be "founded on truth, built on justice, and animated by love."[1] As the Body of Christ on earth, the

Church's mission is to be holy as God is holy. We are to act in such a way that the social realities of economics, politics, industrial and organizational institutions, and cultural communities embody God's justice and compassion.

The Complexity of Contemporary Society

In the United States and in other societies, one individual seldom has the resources to bring about social healing. A solitary minister can hardly begin to address the multiple wounds of even one broken, homeless person. Yet, empowered by the Spirit, a faith community can clothe, shelter, and work with homeless and other persons for long-term solutions to restore dignity and full community participation for all. Alone, we seem powerless. As the People of God working together in Christ's name, we can do more than we hope for or imagine (Eph 3:20).

The Church cannot be a true sign or instrument for effecting God's reign on earth unless communities take collective action together. Lone ministers are quickly overwhelmed and paralyzed by the immensity of our educational, health, and social problems. Yet, those are the very issues that must be addressed if we as workers in the vineyard are to be worth our salt. The evangelization of culture, as Pope Paul tells us in his encyclical *Evangelii nuntiandi,* must bring the full message of the Gospel—the Word of salvation linked with compassionate action on behalf of justice.

Small Christian Communities

As Scripture study groups and other forms of small Christian communities become more immersed in the Gospel and its prophetic roots, their social consciousness begins to change. Often they discover that studying Scripture points to a broader vocation for the adult Christian than they had originally imagined. Group members, especially in long-standing groups, may begin to yearn for a more enlarged purpose and mission for their group, one that includes group action as well as reflection.

Changing the group's purpose requires time for discussion, investigation of options, and planning. One participant may come up with an idea such as, "I think we should consider doing a project or some kind of ministry together," a suggestion which may delight some and surprise others. Time should be set aside at a future meeting to discuss the idea and to determine the level of support for it. If a strong consensus emerges for expanding to action, the group will need further time to consider what an initial project might look like. Even if all members are in agreement that they want to change their scope, they may not have a clear vision as to what that change might entail.

If all members are not prepared to change the group's purpose, a new decision must be made. Will the group continue in its present form or are the needs for change so strong among some of the members that the group may divide into two? Planning should take into account the current task of the group, allowing completion of the current course of study before changes in group life are made. If the change involves the loss or addition of members, further exploration of emotional issues, as mentioned in the earlier sections of this chapter, are in order.

Ministry Projects

Many groups that choose to work in social ministry together begin by taking on some kind of social service project. It may consist of visiting elderly home-bound persons, preparing and serving meals at a local soup kitchen, or collecting clothes for an outreach ministry. These are great starting points and can provide a whole new dimension of community life as members work shoulder to shoulder in service as well as in study and reflection. But another option for a Christian group exists, one that provides a more powerful means of addressing social ills. It involves social *action* as an alternative or in addition to social *service.*

A story tells the tale of a group of friends who, while gathered on the banks of a river, noticed a person in the middle of the river crying for help. With much coordinated effort, they managed to reach the person and bring her to safety. Soon, however, they noticed a second and a third person calling for help in the river. As they reached those, more appeared from upstream. Finally, in exasperation, several of the group decided to leave their companions who were continuing the rescue operation. "How can you leave us now?" they asked. "There are still people in the river calling for help." In reply, the departing companions said, "We're going upstream to find out how they got into the river in the first place."

If we want to effect lasting change that transforms the nature of our society, we must go beyond taking care of casualties. We need to find the root causes of injustices and work toward correcting them. This is the basic work of social action. The ills of our society are complex and the root causes legion, but transformation *is* possible.

Groups who want to join in the work of social action can learn more about how to proceed through resources such as *Social Analysis: Linking Faith and Justice* by Joe Holland and Peter Henriot[2] or by contacting their diocesan social ministry or faith and justice office. A good transitional project for a group that wants to enlarge its purpose beyond Scripture study may be to investigate the resources and options available for social ministry in their area.

Ongoing Need for Scripture Study

Scripture study impels us to make our faith real and alive in both our "private" and "public" lives. We will never outgrow our need to study and reflect on Scripture, and if we listen closely, we will discover in each of our biblical insights a new challenge for conversion and growth. Our Scripture study groups are called to remain open to God's re-creation. We need to pray for openness of mind and heart that through the power of the Spirit and our attention to the Word we will learn what it truly means to be Christian.

SUMMARY

In the course of group life, changes may occur that require the considered attention of the entire group with the help of the facilitator. One of these changes is the introduction of a new member to an existing group. Members need to rework issues that are common to the inclusion phase of group development and to help the new member become assimilated into the ongoing life of the group. The facilitator can assist in this process by helping both the group and new member raise and answer questions that they may have about this transition.

When a group loses a member or when the entire group comes to the end of its life together, feelings of grief and other unresolved emotions often emerge. The group can benefit from time devoted to expressing feelings and reviewing the meaning of the group experience in perspective. The facilitator assists the group in this process by posing questions and listening actively, especially for incomplete expressions of feeling that might be explored in the context of the group.

During the course of the group's life, participants may feel called to expand upon their original purpose for gathering, adding a dimension of community ministry to their ongoing scriptural reflections. In doing so, the group collectively responds to the Church's mission of continuing Jesus' ministry on earth. If we are to become the sacrament of Christ's presence in the world and enable the reign of God to break through in our society, we must take seriously the social teachings of the Church and become a people actively involved in living out God's justice and compassion. Empowered by the Spirit, the concerted efforts of small Christian communities offer a sign of hope for the transformation of society into a world built upon compassion and justice for all.

REMINDER: Read and reflect upon James 2:14-26.

NOTES

1. *Gaudium et Spes: The Pastoral Constitution on the Church in the Modern World* in Walter M. Abbott, ed. and Joseph M. Gallapher, trans., *The Documents of Vatican II* (New York: American Press, 1966) 26.
2. Joe Holland and Peter Henriot, *Social Analysis: Linking Faith and Justice* (Maryknoll: Orbis Books, 1980).

PART B

WORKSHOP SESSIONS

INTRODUCTION

Each of the workshop sessions in Part B presents a design for discussing and practicing the facilitation principles and skills introduced in the corresponding chapter of Part A. The "Learning Objectives" present the overall purpose of the session and name the specific skills that participants will be practicing. The "Session Schedule" gives a general timeline for each of the activities suggested, and the "Session Resources" section provides a more detailed description of each activity. The Workshop Coordinator can modify these designs as needed to meet the specific goals of local groups.

The "Session Resources" section also provides an opening prayer service. Since prayer is an intimate form of expression for each person and community, it is with considerable trepidation that I offer written prayers for use by various groups. The suggested prayers center on scriptural passages that relate in some way to the topic of the workshop session and should be modified or reworked as needed to become the true prayer expression of the community.

When two sessions are combined into one three-hour session, the "closing prayer" of the first session and the "opening prayer" of the second session can be combined or omitted, allowing the group to take a break between the two sessions.

Participants should bring this book and their Bibles to each session.

WORKSHOP SESSION 1
THE ROLE OF GROUP FACILITATOR

LEARNING OBJECTIVES

By the end of this session, participants will be able to:

- describe the role of a facilitator in a Scripture study or faith-sharing group.
- describe some of the characteristics of an effective facilitator.

SESSION SCHEDULE

Activity	Time
Opening Prayer	05
Introductions	10
Small-Group Discussion	40
Assessment Instrument	10
Assessment Discussion	15
Large-Group Discussion	10
Assignments and Closing Prayer	05
	90 minutes

SESSION RESOURCES

Opening Prayer

Song: (to be announced)

Leader: God of Abraham and Sarah, God of Mary and Joseph, Abba of Jesus and our God, we Your People raise our hearts and minds to You, seeking your guidance as we listen to your Word in Scripture. May your life-giving Word become a reality in our lives that through your Spirit we may help to renew the face of the earth.

All: Loving God, you sustain us as a People and nourish us with your life, help us to hear and understand your Word spoken new to us this day. Guide us in our reflections and in our caring for one another that we may become a sign of your love to others throughout our lives.

Reader: Luke 22:24-27.
Pause for reflection.

Leader: Let us conclude our prayer with the *Magnificat* (Luke 1:46-55).

Left: My soul magnifies the LORD,
and my spirit rejoices in God my Savior
who has looked with favor on me, a lowly serving maid.

Right: From this day all generations will call me blessed.
The Mighty One has done great things for me;
holy the name of the Lord,
whose mercy is on the God-fearing
from generation to generation.

Left: The arm of the Lord is filled with strength,
scattering the proudhearted.

Right: God hurled the mighty from their thrones,
lifting up the lowly.

Left: God filled the hungry with good things,
            sending the rich away empty.
            God has come to the help of Israel, the Lord's servant,

Right: remembering mercy,
            the mercy promised to our forebears,
            to Abraham and his children forever.

All: Amen.

Introductions

Since this is primarily intended to be the first in a series of workshops, time is scheduled here to invite each participant to introduce himself or herself. Even if participants know one another from other settings, they might be invited to share, for example, one significant memory in their experience of facilitating or a goal they would like to achieve through the ongoing facilitator training. If the workshop group is very large (more than sixteen people), participants might introduce themselves in smaller groups.

Discussion Questions for Small Group

Join with four or five other persons to discuss the three questions prepared as Warm-Up Exercises for Chapter 1 (see pages 15–16). Then, discuss the additional two questions:

a. How does Luke's image of leadership relate to your image of a group facilitator?

b. What parts of the facilitator role seem to be fairly easy for you to assume? What parts of the role are most challenging? Why?

Assessment Instrument

Facilitation skills in groups are shared by many participants. The "Discussion Assessment Instrument" found on page 125 lists some of the skills that generally help to facilitate group discussions. See if you can identify who in your group contributed any of the listed skills during your small-group discussion (described above). List names only if you can recall a specific instance of the person contributing that skill in your discussion.

DISCUSSION ASSESSMENT INSTRUMENT

Facilitation Skill

Names of Group Members
(*use initials or abbreviate*)

1. Posed the discussion question   _____

2. Shared responses to questions   _____

3. Restated what another was saying in order to clarify   _____

4. Asked for more information or
   meaning from another member   _____

5. Named feelings as well as
   thoughts   _____

6. Built upon another's ideas   _____

7. Connected comments made by
   one person with comments
   made by another   _____

8. Harmonized two opposing
   views or offered a compromise
   view   _____

9. Made room for another speaker
   to enter into the discussion   _____

10. Injected humor at an appropri-
    ate time   _____

11. Observed what the group as a
    whole or what another seemed
    to be feeling   _____

12. Directed the group back to the
    topic of conversation   _____

Assessment Discussion

Using the Assessment Instrument you just completed, discuss what you observed taking place in your earlier discussion with members of your group. Point out any contributions members made that you thought were particularly helpful to the group discussion.

Large-Group Discussion

Share any insights you gained from this session on the role of facilitator with others in the large group.

Assignments and Closing Prayer

If the group will be meeting for another session, review the chapter (in Part A of this book) for that session. Then, close this session with the Lord's Prayer.

WORKSHOP SESSION 2
GETTING STARTED

LEARNING OBJECTIVES

By the end of this session, participants will be able to:

• describe some of the ways to create a climate in which members can feel at ease with one another in a newly forming group.

• describe some of the group norms that strengthen the healthy functioning of a discussion group.

SESSION SCHEDULE

Activity	Time
Opening Prayer	05
Review of Group Agreement	20
Group Discussion 1	30
Group Discussion 2	15
Assessment of Discussion	15
Assignments and Closing Prayer	05
	90 minutes

SESSION RESOURCES

Opening Prayer

Song: (to be announced)
        Suggestion: "Gather Us In"

Leader: Loving God, you are the Source of all life. In you we find
        our beginnings and the deepest longings of our hearts. Help
        us as we ponder how communities are born that we might
        see your love as the source of all of our friendships and
        social nourishment. May we be one in your Spirit. We ask
        this in Christ our Lord.

All: Amen.

Reader: Ephesians 2:12-22.
        Pause for reflection.

Leader: Let us voice our thanks and petitions:
        The response is: Lord, hear our prayer.

Participants: (Share petitions with the group.)

Leader: With hearts joined, we commend these and all of the stir-
        rings of our hearts to you. Lead us in your path that we
        may grow in justice, faith, and solidarity with all of our
        brothers and sisters and fellow creatures of the earth. In
        Jesus name we pray.

All: Amen.

Review of Group Agreement

In groups of five to eight participants, review the sample **Group
Agreement** found on page 36. Use the following questions to guide
the discussion of these norms as guidelines for your own group in
this workshop:

  1. Are there any norms listed in the agreement that seem chal-
    lenging or troublesome to you? If so, which ones?

2. What suggestions do you have for any additional norms that should be included?

3. What advantages and disadvantages do you see to having a written group agreement when starting a new group?

Group Discussion 1

Continuing in the same group, discuss the three questions that you completed in your Warm-Up Exercises for Chapter 2.

Group Discussion 2

Rearrange the chairs of your group so that all chairs are in a straight line side-by-side except for one (at least four chairs should be in the line). The other chair should directly face the line-up of chairs (See Figure 2.1). Now, begin discussing the questions listed below while your group maintains this seating arrangement (about five minutes). After that, the group should re-form in a circular seating arrangement and continue with its discussion. The discussion questions are:

1. Reflecting on the reading from Ephesians (2:12-22): In what ways have you experienced the movement from being strangers to being joined together with others in Christ?

2. What implications does this passage have for the way you join with others in Christian community?

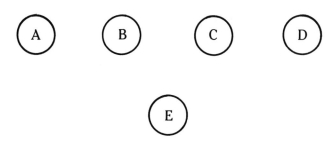

Figure 2.1 Seating Arrangement

Assessment of Discussion

In the total group of participants, rearrange the chairs into a circle and discuss your experiences in the previous experiment.

1. What effect did the seating arrangement have on your discussion?

2. What do you consider to be the most important things for a facilitator to keep in mind when starting a new group?

Assignments and Closing Prayer

If the group will be meeting for another session, review the chapter (in Part A of this book) for that session. Then, close this session with the Lord's Prayer.

WORKSHOP SESSION 3
COMMUNICATION BASICS—
EXPRESSIVE SKILLS

LEARNING OBJECTIVES

By the end of this session, participants will be able to:

- describe some of the expressive skills that help to build an atmosphere of trust and respect in a group.
- demonstrate a variety of expressive skills.

SESSION SCHEDULE

Activity	Time
Opening Prayer	05
Discussion of Readings	30
Skills Exercise in Triads	30
Large-Group Discussion	20
Assignments and Closing Prayer	05
	90 minutes

SESSION RESOURCES

Opening Prayer

Song: (to be announced)

Leader: Let us bring to mind the presence of God in our lives.
(Pause for a brief quiet time).
Together let us join in praying Psalm 34.

Left: I will bless the LORD at all times;
praise shall always be in my mouth.

Right: My soul will glory in the LORD
that the poor may hear and be glad.

Left: Magnify the LORD with me;
let us exalt his name together.

Right: I sought the LORD, who answered me,
delivered me from all my fears.

Left: Look to God that you may be radiant with joy
and your faces may not blush for shame.

Right: In my misfortune I called,
the LORD heard and saved me from all distress.

Left: The angel of the LORD, who encamps with them,
delivers all who fear God.

Right: Learn to savor how good the LORD is;
happy are those who take refuge in him.

Left: Fear the LORD, you his holy ones;
nothing is lacking to those who fear him. . . .

Right: Come, children, listen to me;
I will teach you the fear of the LORD.

Left: Who among you loves life,
takes delight in prosperous days?

Right: Keep your tongue from evil,
       your lips from speaking lies.

Left: Turn from evil and do good;
       seek peace and pursue it.

Reading: Jeremiah 1:4-10.
       Pause for reflection.

Leader: We thank you, our God, for the many expressions of your life and love that surround us. You communicate your very Self to us and have created us to express your love to others.

All: We thank you also for gifts of our own consciousness and self-expression. May we ever proclaim your love and justice and may your praises be ever on our lips. As we join in community with others, help us to express clearly the inmost thoughts of our hearts with one another that we may be one in you. And grant that we may use your gifts wisely for the work of your justice and peace on earth. We ask this through Christ our Lord. Amen.

Discussion Questions for Small Group

Join with four or five other persons to discuss the following questions:

1. Of the expressive skills mentioned in the assigned essay, which do you feel are your current strengths and which do you most need to improve?

2. What other skills would you add to the list provided in the readings? State why you consider these additional skills to be important.

3. What are some specific ways in which the facilitator of a group can assist others to express themselves more congruently, respectfully, and clearly?

Skills Exercise in Triads

Form groups of three persons each (some may be composed of four persons, if necessary). Each person in the group will be given approximately eight minutes to share on the two questions prepared as Warm-Up Exercises for Chapter 3 (see page 37).

In the triads assign one person to be Person A, another to be Person B, and the third as Person C (See Figure 3.1.). There will be three rounds to allow each person in the triad to take a "speaking" role.

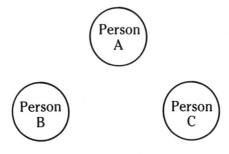

Figure 3.1 Seating Arrangement

Round 1:   **Person A** in the group is the "speaker," sharing answers prepared for the "Warm-Up" questions on page 37.

Person B in the group is the "listener," asking follow-up questions if he or she chooses.

Person C in the group is the "observer" and should take notes on the Person A's (1) use of I-language, (2) concreteness in expression, and (3) expressions of feeling, both verbal and non-verbal.

After the eight minutes are up, the observer (Person C) should give feedback to Person A and lead a *two-minute* discussion with the other two on Person A's pattern of self-expression. After the review is completed, go on to Round 2.

Round 2: Person B is the speaker.
Person C is the listener.
Person A is the observer.

Again, spend about two minutes reviewing the speaker's use of expressive skills. Then, go on to Round 3.

Round 3: Person C is the speaker.
Person A is the listener.
Person B is the observer.

Remember to watch the time so that each person gets a chance to take all three roles. (In groups of four the sharing time may be cut to five minutes to allow each person time to express their reflections. Two persons will take the role of observer in each round.)

Large-Group Discussion

Participants should reflect on the questions listed below and share any new insights they may have gained as a result of the triad exercise.

- Which expressive skills did you most often observe in the three rounds?

- Which skills did you least often observe?

Assignments and Closing Prayer

If the group will be meeting for another session, review the chapter (in Part A of this book) for that session. Then, close this session with the spontaneous prayers of group members followed by the Lord's Prayer. One member of the group should act as presider of the closing prayer, inviting the group to gather in a circle and beginning the shared prayer.

WORKSHOP SESSION 4
COMMUNICATION BASICS—
LISTENING SKILLS

LEARNING OBJECTIVES

By the end of this session, participants will be able to:

• describe the purpose and skills involved in active listening.

• demonstrate a variety of active listening skills.

SESSION SCHEDULE

Activity	Time
Opening Prayer	05
Discussion of Readings	30
Skills Exercise in Triads	40
Large-Group Discussion	10
Assignments and Closing Prayer	05
	90 minutes

SESSION RESOURCES

Opening Prayer

Song: (to be announced)

Leader: Let us listen as we recite Psalm 81:8-15, 17.

Left: 'Listen, my people, I give you warning!
             If only you will obey me, Israel!

Right: There must be no foreign god among you;
             you must not worship an alien god.

Left: I, the LORD, am your God,
             who brought you up from the land of Egypt.
             Open wide your mouth that I may fill it.'

Right: But my people did not listen to my words;
             Israel did not obey me.

Left: So I gave them over to hardness of heart;
             they followed their own designs.

Right: But even now if my people would listen,
             if Israel would walk in my paths,

Left: In a moment I would subdue their foes,
             against their enemies unleash my hand. . . .

Right: But Israel I would feed with the finest wheat,
             satisfy them with honey from the rock.

Reading: Acts 15:1-12.
           Pause for reflection.

Leader: Let us voice the prayers of our hearts to our God who
             listens to us. The response is: "Hear us, O Lord."

Participants: (Voice their prayers.)

Leader: Loving Friend and Creator of the universe, we thank you
             for speaking you call to us in so many ways. We thank

you also for listening to the prayers of our hearts. Open our ears that we may hear you and others more clearly. Open our eyes that we may see you in the faces of our brothers and sisters and in the beauty of creation. May we always listen to your Word and respond to it with our lives. We ask this in Jesus' name.

All: Amen.

Discussion Questions for Small Group

Join with four or five other persons to discuss the following questions:

1. How would you describe the purpose and effect of active listening?

2. Based upon your own experiences and on the reading assignment, in what ways can a facilitator and group participants use active listening to further a discussion? Give some examples from your own experience.

3. Based upon your own experiences and on the reading assignment, when might some active listening response not be helpful in a group discussion? Give some examples from your own experience.

Skills Exercise in Triads

Form groups of three persons each (some may be composed of four persons if necessary). Each person in the group will be given approximately *ten minutes* to share on the questions prepared as Warm-Up Exercises (see pages 47–48) for Chapter 4. (In groups of four, eight minutes per person would allow each person to have practice time. Two persons will take the role of observer in each round.)

In the triads, assign one person to be Person A, another to be Person B, and the third as Person C (See Figure 4.1.).

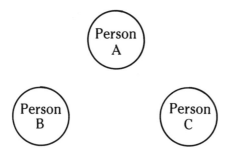

Figure 4.1 Seating Arrangement

Round 1: **Person A** in the group is the "speaker," sharing answers prepared for the "Warm-Up" questions on pages 47–48.

Person B in the group is the "listener," demonstrating active listening skills follow-up questions if he or she chooses.

Person C in the group is the "observer" and should take notes on the Person B's (1) use of various reflective responses (reflecting explicit content, underlying feelings, or implications), (2) use of probing statements (questions and directives), and (3) non-verbal behavior.

After the ten minutes are up, the observer (Person C) should give feedback to Person B and lead a *three-minute* discussion with the other two on Person B's pattern of listening. Then, go on to Round 2.

Round 2: Person B is the speaker.
Person C is the listener.
Person A is the observer.

Again, spend three minutes reviewing the listener's use of active listening skills, and go on to Round 3.

Round 3: Person C is the speaker.
Person A is the listener.
Person B is the observer.

Remember to watch the time so that each person gets a chance to take all three roles.

Large-Group Discussion

Share any new insights that participants may have gained as a result of the triad exercise. Which skills were most often observed? Which skills were least often observed?

Assignments and Closing Prayer

If the group will be meeting for another session, review the chapter (in Part A of this book) for that session. Then, close this session with the spontaneous prayers of group members followed by the Lord's Prayer. One member of the group should act as presider of the closing prayer, inviting the group to gather in a circle and beginning the shared prayer.

WORKSHOP SESSION 5
CONNECTING SCRIPTURE
WITH LIFE EXPERIENCES

LEARNING OBJECTIVES

By the end of this session, participants will be able to:

• distinguish various types of discussion questions.

• describe some of the ways to help participants connect the meaning of Scripture with their own life circumstances, experiences, and responses.

SESSION SCHEDULE

Activity	Time
Opening Prayer	05
Question Development Exercise	15
Small-Group Discussion	45
Large-Group Discussion	20
Assignments and Closing Prayer	05
	90 minutes

SESSION RESOURCES

Opening Prayer

Song: (to be announced)

Leader: Lord, you teach us that "one does not live by bread alone, but by every word that comes from the mouth of God." We pray that your Word may feed us and enliven us to become the persons of holiness you call us to be.

All: May we be open to hearing your Word spoken through Scripture and through the everyday events of our lives.

From Psalm 119

Left: With all my heart I seek you;
    do not let me stray from your commands.
In my heart treasure your promise,
    that I may not sin against you.

Right: Blessed are you, O LORD;
    teach me your laws.
With my lips I recite
    all the edicts you have spoken.

Left: I find joy in the way of your decrees
    more than in all riches.
I will ponder your precepts
    and consider your paths. . . .

Right: Be kind to your servant that I may live,
    that I may keep your word.
Open my eyes to see clearly
    the wonders of your teachings. . . .

Left: Let your love come to me, LORD,
    salvation in accord with your promise.

Right: Let me answer my taunters with a word,
    for I trust in your word. . . .

Left: How sweet to my tongue is your promise,
           sweeter than honey to my mouth! . . .

Right: Your word is a lamp for my feet,
           a light for my path . . .
           Accept my freely offered praise;
           LORD, teach me your decrees.

Reading: Luke 10:25-37.
           This is the word of the Lord.

All: Thanks be to God.

Question Development Exercise

In groups of four or five, review one another's questions developed in each of the five categories presented in the *Question Development Exercise* on pages 71–72. Check that the questions composed and presented by each participant are actual examples of the intended category. You may not have time to review every example of each participant, but try to review a few questions from each of the five categories.

Small-Group Discussion

Continuing in groups of four or five, each participant will take a turn in posing a question to the group for discussion. The first person will pose a question of *Fact* (from the sample questions or from his or her own composition) related to Luke 10:25-37. After the group has had time to discuss the question, the next person will pose a question of *Concretizing* for group discussion. The third will pose a question of *Meaning;* the fourth person, a question of *Balance;* and the fifth, a question of *Response.* Each time a question is posed, the group should discuss and share their responses, engaging in active listening and further probing with one another as the dialogue warrants it. If time remains, the group may begin a second round of questions in the same order until the end of the forty-five minute discussion period.

Large-Group Discussion

The entire group should form a circle and consider the following questions:

1. In your small-group discussions, what kinds of questions stimulated discussion the best?

2. How does your experience of discussion questions here compare with the one you recalled in your Warm-Up Exercises?

3. What have you learned about the use of questions in linking personal experiences with the lessons of Scripture?

Assignments and Closing Prayer

If the group will be meeting for another session, review the chapter (in Part A of this book) for that session. Then, close this session with the Lord's Prayer.

WORKSHOP SESSION 6
INTEGRATING OUR DIVERSITY

LEARNING OBJECTIVES

By the end of this session, participants will be able to:

- describe some of the ways that diversity affects their current group interactions.
- identify ways of challenging members to uphold healthy group norms.

SESSION SCHEDULE

Activity	Time
Opening Prayer	05
Large-Group Discussion	40
Small-Group Discussion	20
Large-Group Discussion	20
Assignments and Closing Prayer	05
	90 minutes

SESSION RESOURCES

Opening Prayer

Song: (to be announced)

Leader: Let us open our minds and hearts to our God who is ever-present to us.

From Psalm 95

Left: Come, let us sing joyfully to the LORD;
cry out to the rock of our salvation.

Right: Let us greet him with a song of praise
joyfully sing out our psalms. . . .

All: Enter, let us bow down in worship;
let us kneel before the LORD who made us.

Leader: Let us voice the prayers of our hearts.

Participants: (share their own prayers)

Leader: God of Love, we seek you with all our hearts. We bring before you these our prayers of hope and thanksgiving. May you shine through us as we bring the hope of your salvation to our world.

Reading: 1 Corinthians 12:12-26.
This is the Word of the Lord.

All: Thanks be to God.

Large-Group Discussion

Begin by discussing responses to the two questions posed for reflection in the Warm-Up Exercises for Chapter 6 (page 73), along with any questions or comments on the readings that participants may have. Then, post on newsprint the personality preference profiles of participants in the group. Consider the following questions for discussion:

1. How well do the profiles of members in the group comple-
ment one another? In terms of personality profiles, which profiles or dimension scores predominate in the group?

2. How do the differences among members affect the tone and
direction of discussion in the group?

Small-Group Discussion

In small groups of four or five, review participants' responses
to the **Group Situations Exercise** on pages 90–91. One member of
the small group should note any questions or disagreements on the
appropriateness of responses and be prepared to report these to the
total group.

Large-Group Discussion

Share any questions or insights that arose in the small group review of the **Group Situations Exercise.** Then, consider the following questions for discussion:

1. What does 1 Corinthians 12:12-26 say to you about diversity
in the Christian community?

2. What are some of the ways that group members can affirm
and respect the uniqueness of their fellow participants?

Assignments and Closing Prayer

If the group will be meeting for another session, review the chapter (in Part A of this book) for that session. Then, close this session
with the spontaneous prayers of group members followed by the
Lord's Prayer. One member of the group should act as presider of
the closing prayer, inviting the group to gather in a circle and beginning the shared prayer.

WORKSHOP SESSION 7
TUNING INTO GROUP LIFE

LEARNING OBJECTIVES

By the end of this session, participants will be able to:

• describe ways of assessing group life as a whole.

• observe a variety of facilitative behaviors in a group.

SESSION SCHEDULE

Activity	Time
Opening Prayer	05
Small-Group Discussion	20
Decision Exercise	30
Discussion of Exercise	20
Large-Group Discussion	10
Assignments and Closing Prayer	05
	90 minutes

SESSION RESOURCES

Opening Prayer

Song: (to be announced)

Leader: Let us gather as one in the presence of the Lord.

All: We thank you, O God, our Creator and Redeemer, for bringing us together as one People, formed in your love and compassion. We praise you for the wonder of our lives. We praise you for the wonders of community where our lives are enriched and made whole. Help us to heal one another's brokenness and to be sources of your graceful presence to all.

Reader: Ephesians 4:1-6.
Pause for reflection.

Leader: Let us bring our prayers of petition and thanksgiving before the Lord.

All: (Participants are invited to share prayers openly with the group.) The response is, "Lord, hear our prayer."

Leader: Gracious God, we entrust these our prayers into your care. May our faith and trust in you increase, and may our compassion and response to our sisters and brothers deepen in your Spirit.
We ask this through Christ our Lord.

All: Amen.

Small-Group Discussion

In groups of four or five participants, review answers to the questions prepared as Warm-Up Exercises for Chapter 7 (see page 92). Then, discuss the following questions:

    a. What in the readings helped you to clarify some of the ways you can help a group to grow?

b. What questions do you still have about facilitating group progress?

Decision Exercise

This exercise involves two different tasks, one for "participants" and the other for "observers" of the exercises. Participants will practice communication skills as they work toward a consensus decision (see page 101 in Chapter 7). Observers will practice observation skills and will record which facilitation skills are demonstrated by the participants. The categories used on the Observation Form are those described on pages 100–103 in Chapter 7.

Five or six "participants" are needed for the Decision Exercise; they should sit in a circle in the center of the room. Everyone else will take the role of "observer" and sit in an outer circle so that they observe the "inner" circle of participants (See Figure 7.1.). Allow everyone to arrange their seats before proceeding with the task.

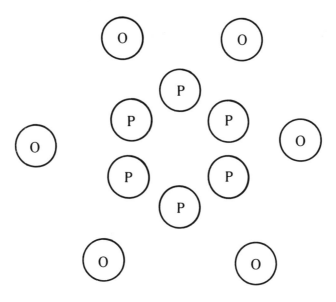

Figure 7.1 Seating Arrangement for Decision Excercise

Participants in the Decision Exercise have the following task:

1. Several potential group problems are listed on the **Potential Group Problems List** on page 153. Each participant should take two to three minutes to rank the problems in order of the most difficult to deal with (#1) to the least difficult to deal with (#8).

2. When each participant has completed the individual ranking, the participant group should discuss the list of potential problems and reach a consensus decision on the rank order of the problems in terms of their difficulty.

Observers in the Decision Exercise have the following task:

1. List the names of the participants at the top of the Observation Form (page 154).

2. During the participants' discussion of how to rank the list, Observers should make a tally mark (/) in the appropriate category each time someone in the group demonstrates a facilitative behavior listed on the Observation Form. (Almost every time someone speaks, a tally mark should be made.)

POTENTIAL GROUP PROBLEMS LIST

Directions: Place a "1" next to the problem you think is most difficult to deal with in a group, a "2" next to the next most difficult, etc. The least difficult problem should receive a ranking of "8."

_____ A. A group member who tells long stories with much detail

_____ B. A member who continually wants to convince others of a particular viewpoint

_____ C. A person who interrupts others before they finish speaking

_____ D. Discussion questions that don't stimulate much discussion

_____ E. Running out of time in the middle of a good discussion

_____ F. A person who often brings up and reflects upon personal problems at length

_____ G. A quiet member who rarely says anything

_____ H. A member who walks in 15 minutes late to each meeting

OBSERVATION FORM

Directions: List the names of the Decision Exercise Participants in the spaces provided. Each time a participant demonstrates one of the facilitative behaviors listed below, record it with a tally mark (/) in the appropriate space below their name.

Participant Names: |_____|_____|_____|_____|_____|

Task Behaviors

Initiating |_____|_____|_____|_____|_____|

Providing Information |_____|_____|_____|_____|_____|

Seeking Information |_____|_____|_____|_____|_____|

Clarifying/Elaborating |_____|_____|_____|_____|_____|

Summarizing |_____|_____|_____|_____|_____|

Consensus Testing |_____|_____|_____|_____|_____|

Maintenance Behaviors

Gatekeeping |_____|_____|_____|_____|_____|

Encouraging |_____|_____|_____|_____|_____|

Harmonizing |_____|_____|_____|_____|_____|

Expressing group
feelings |_____|_____|_____|_____|_____|

Pointing out
communication
patterns |_____|_____|_____|_____|_____|

Standard setting |_____|_____|_____|_____|_____|

Discussion of Exercise

Participants in the Decision Exercise should begin the discussion by commenting on their experiences in the exercise. Consider the following questions:

- What was helpful in moving the discussion and decision-making process along?

- What seemed to hinder or block progress in the group?

- Who in the group emerged as prime facilitator?

Observers should then report what they had recorded.

- Who in the group engaged most in task-oriented behaviors?

- Who in the group engaged most in maintenance behaviors?

- What facilitative behaviors or skills were needed but were not demonstrated in the group?

- What norms seemed to be operating in the group? (See pages 94–97).

- How well did the group function and why?

Large-Group Discussion

After the group has analyzed the Decision Exercise itself, everyone involved in the session is invited to discuss the following questions:

a. Based upon your experiences in groups, which of the facilitative skills (task-oriented and maintenance behaviors) listed on the Observation Form seem to be the most important for maintaining a healthy group life?

b. Are there any other important facilitative skills that are not listed on the Observation Form? Discuss these.

Assignments and Closing Prayer

If the group will be meeting for another session, review the chapter (in Part A of this book) for that session. Then, close this session with the spontaneous prayers of group members followed by the Lord's Prayer. One member of the group should act as presider of the closing prayer, inviting the group to gather in a circle and beginning the shared prayer.

If you are going on to Session 8, please note that since it is the last session of the workshop, time is allotted for a special closing prayer to be prepared by some of the participants. A celebration with refreshments might also be in order. The group may want to identify volunteers for these activities.

WORKSHOP SESSION 8
GROUP TRANSITIONS

LEARNING OBJECTIVES

By the end of this session, participants will be able to:

- name some of the issues that might arise for groups in different kinds of transition.
- describe some of the ways to help groups move successfully through times of transition.

SESSION SCHEDULE

Activity	Time
Opening Prayer	05
Small-Group Discussion	20
Large-Group Discussion	45
Closing Prayer and Celebration	20
	90 minutes

SESSION RESOURCES

Opening Prayer

Song: (to be announced at the session)

Leader: Let us open our hearts and minds to the Word of God.

(Isaiah 58:5-10)

Left: Is such the fast that I choose,
            a day for people to humble themselves?
            Is it to bow down their head like a rush,
            and to spread sackcloth and ashes under them?

Right: Will you call this a fast,
            and a day acceptable to the Lord?

Left: Is not this the fast that I choose:
            to loose the bonds of wickedness,
            to undo the thongs of the yoke,

Right: to let the oppressed go free,
            and to break every yoke?

Left: Is it not to share your bread with the hungry,
            and bring the homeless poor into your house;

Right: when you see the naked, to cover them,
            and not to hide yourselves from your own flesh?

Left: Then shall your light break fourth like the dawn,
            and your healing shall spring up speedily;

Right: your righteousness shall go before you,
            the glory of the Lord shall be your rear guard.

Left: Then you shall call, and the Lord will answer;
            you shall cry, and God will say, Here I am.

Right: If you take away from the midst of you the yoke,
            the pointing of the finger, and speaking wickedness,

Left: if you pour yourselves out for the hungry
        and satisfy the desire of the afflicted,

Right: then shall your light rise in the darkness
        and your gloom be as the noonday.

Reader: James 2:14-26.
        Pause for reflection.

Leader: Let us bring our prayers to our God who is full of compassion and longs for justice.

All: (Participants are invited to share prayers openly with the group.) The response is, "Lord, hear our prayer."

Leader: Merciful God, we bring these and all of the unspoken prayers of our hearts to you. We ask for your transforming grace in our lives that we may become Christ for others and we ask this in the name of Jesus our Lord,

All: Amen.

Small-Group Discussion

In groups of four or five participants, review answers to the following questions prepared as Warm-Up Exercises for Chapter 8 (see pages 105–106):

  a. What experiences have you had with times of transition in the life of a group (e.g., loss or addition of a member, end of group, etc.)? What helped or hindered the group in those moments?

  b. Read James 2:14-26. What challenges do you hear in this passage for faith-sharing communities?

Then, discuss the following question:

  c. What points in the session essay did you find helpful for facilitating groups during times of transition?

Large-Group Discussion

In the total group setting, discuss the remaining questions prepared as Warm-Up Exercises for Chapter 8:

a. What have you learned as a result of these sessions that will help you most as a facilitator?

b. How might this learning experience apply to other relationships in your life?

c. What questions do you still have about facilitating groups?

d. How will you continue to gather information and develop the facilitation skills you need?

Closing Prayer

Those who have prepared the closing prayer service should lead the closing service. A celebration with refreshments should follow.